DREAM DIFFERENTLY

Dream
Differently

Candid Advice for America's Students

Dr. Vince M. Bertram

NEW YORK TIMES BESTSELLING AUTHOR

REGNERY
PUBLISHING
A Division of Salem Media Group

Regnery® is a registered trademark of Salem Communications Holding Corporation

Cataloging-in-Publication data on file with the Library of Congress

First ebook edition 2017: ISBN 978-1-62157-693-8
Orignally published in hardcover, 2017: ISBN 978-1-62157-678-5

Published in the United States by
Regnery Publishing
A Division of Salem Media Group
300 New Jersey Ave NW
Washington, DC 20001
www.Regnery.com

Manufactured in the United States of America

10 9 8 7 6 5 4 3 2 1

Books are available in quantity for promotional or premium use. For information on discounts and terms, please visit our website: www.Regnery.com.

Distributed to the trade by
Perseus Distribution
www.perseusdistribution.com

Contents

ONE

The Three Questions

A young man I work with once told me a story about how he was taught in high school. "One day in my high school trigonometry class, a fellow student asked our teacher, 'Ms. Winston, why do we need to learn this?' She thought for a moment and replied, 'In case you become a high school math teacher.'"

You may have had a similar experience, sitting in your trigonometry or biology or chemistry class and wondering, "When will I *ever* use this?" Despite what your annoyed teacher might say, it's a fair question. Teachers should be able to tell students why they study certain subjects, although I don't suggest putting them on the spot in the middle of a lesson. And, no, it's not just in case you become a teacher yourself one day.

Another common answer—"because it will make you an educated person"—is equally unsatisfying. Certainly you want to be an educated person, but as you look around, you see plenty of educated people who never use trig, or calculus, or chemistry at all. Whatever they might have learned about those subjects during school, they've certainly forgotten by now.

True, there are thousands upon thousands of jobs you could get that will never ever ask you to do long division, much less algebra or calculus. There are thousands upon thousands of jobs that will never test your knowledge of circuit breakers or chemical compositions. There are thousands upon thousands of jobs that will never ask you to know a single line of computer code or decipher reams of raw data.

And yet, according to the National Association of Colleges and Employers, engineering and math fields dominate the list of college majors that employers are looking for in job applicants. Finance and accounting ranked No. 1 and No. 2, followed by computer science (No. 3), mechanical engineering (No. 4), business administration (No. 5), electrical engineering (No. 6), and information sciences and systems (No. 7).

And not only that—these careers are also among the best for making a difference in the world, whether you dream of reviving the space program, curing cancer, addressing climate change, or designing the next-generation Apple Watch.

Want to be a game developer? You'll need to understand trigonometry.

Want to be an engineer, architect, health care professional, or even a musician? Many careers in those fields use trigonometry on a regular basis.

But you may not know that, because the way many U.S. high schools approach subjects like trigonometry focuses more on the calculations than on the applications. Too often, we tell students like you that you'll need to know trigonometry if you become a high school math teacher, or because it's going to be on the test, which we demonstrate by teaching rigid lessons on sine, cosine, and tangent formulas.

Although there are a host of reasons we approach education this way, it ultimately does a great disservice to students because it fails to help them develop a real appreciation for how subjects like trig apply to the real world. In all of the professions mentioned above, it's almost always more important to understand the principles of trig—and what their use can tell you about the world—than it is to know the equations by heart or to be able to calculate them in your head. That's what calculators are for.

In fact, it's increasingly important for job seekers to have at least a basic understanding of trigonometry and other science, technology, engineering, and math (STEM) fields. By 2018, jobs in STEM fields are expected to grow at a rate nearly double those of other fields—17 percent versus 9.8 percent.[1] An estimated 1.2 million STEM jobs will go unfilled because the workforce will not possess the skills to fill them.

My purpose is not to push you towards a STEM career. For reasons we'll get into later, I believe that having a firm foundation in STEM subjects is just a smart thing to do. But you may have different dreams, and I don't intend to dissuade you from pursuing them.

What I do intend to do is provide you with information, perspective, and a few questions that, if answered honestly, will help you plot out an educational and career pathway that will help you achieve your dreams.

This is a book about college, but we're not going to talk about college just yet. Instead, we're going to talk about dreams—specifically, your dreams. Think back to when you were young—around eight or nine—and an adult asked you, "What do you want to be when you grow up?"

Do you remember your answer? If you're like most people, whatever you thought you wanted to be when you were eight or nine has likely changed. With age comes wisdom, and you're now wise enough to know that your childhood dream of being Batman was a bit misguided. So, how would you answer the question today? What do you want to be when you grow up? What do you want to do with your life?

If you don't know how you would answer that question, keep reading!

If you do know what you want to do with your life, congratulations! You're already a step ahead of many of your peers. But the questions get more difficult from here. How confident are you that your current career goals, ambitions, and desires are more attainable than your earlier dreams? Do you have a plan to make your dreams a reality?

There's no right or wrong answer here. I'm not telling you that your dreams are wrong or misguided. But I want you to think about them in a serious way, because I'm going to guess no one has really asked you to before. In fact, my guess is that much of what you've heard from teachers, counselors, and speakers comes down to some variation of "Follow your dreams." I should know, because I work with young adults like you every day.

"Follow your dreams" is a nice sentiment, but—just like the traditional answers to questions like "why must we learn this?"—it does you a great disservice because it fails to challenge you to examine your dreams and develop a plan for achieving them. My goal for this book is to get you thinking about how to follow your dreams *in a smart way*, whether you dream of becoming a superstar mathematician or superstar athlete.

Perhaps you're very good at STEM subjects in school. Or perhaps you're much better at their counterparts in the humanities, which include social studies, English and other languages, and history. Most people tend to gravitate to one or the other.

You're going to hear a lot about STEM subjects and careers in the pages that follow. It's a field that I know well and that I believe more students should study. But I'm also serious when I say that I don't want to push you in any career direction. I'm not suggesting that you ignore your dreams and become an engineer. What's most important is that you have an understanding and appreciation of how your education—past and future—is relevant in real life. This applies to STEM as well as to the humanities.

For example, let's say you're very good at STEM subjects—so good, in fact, that your dream is to work at Google or a similar tech giant. Before you ditch the humanities entirely, just listen to what a Google executive recently told me: "If there is one skill that I never imagined would be so important in what I do and the success I've achieved, it's writing. Even though I really didn't understand at the time what those classes were going to do for me in the future…actually struggling to get the Bs that I got in those classes turned out to be pretty valuable, because I write all the time today. It's so important to my work that I write well."

Starting to get the idea? Even STEM experts need to know how to write. Would you take your English courses a bit more seriously if you knew how valuable writing would be to your future? This is exactly what I mean by following your dreams *in a smart way*. My goal is to show you the importance of having a plan for your career.

Yes, I said *career*. At this stage of life it may be very difficult to see much beyond college, but you should be thinking seriously about your career. And in the first part of this book, we're going to start with a simple question: *What is your dream*?

Next, we'll move to the world economy you will enter when you leave college. This world is full of opportunities and excitement, as well as hardships and dead ends. The question you need to be able to answer is: *Will you be ready for this rapidly evolving world*?

After that, we'll finally tackle the subject of college. We're going to look at how to choose the right school, how to choose the right major, and what else you should be doing while you're there. At the end of this section, you should be able to answer another simple question: *What do you want to get out of college*?

College doesn't exist just to give you "the college experience." College is a means to an end; it exists to prepare you for what you want to become after college. Yet far too many students enter college with no real understanding of what they want to do after graduation—or even what awaits them beyond the campus. How can you prepare for something you don't see or understand?

You can't. That's why I wrote this book for you: to help you see what's awaiting you, especially because you may not want to see it, yet. You may be thinking that right now you have a few years to enjoy before "real life" begins, and seriously planning for the future may be the last thing on your mind. But it is in your best interest to approach college with a plan, an idea of what you want to get out of it.

I want to help you put that plan together. I won't lecture you; rather, my goal is to expand your horizons a bit. I want to help you think about college, and life after college, in ways you probably haven't considered. I want you to think beyond your dreams, because they may actually be limiting you. Maybe it's not that your dreams are too big; it may be that they're too narrow. You may not know yet all the ways you could follow your dreams and achieve them.

So, I'm going to introduce you to some former students who, much like you, didn't know that their dreams were limiting them. But when they expanded their horizons and stepped out of their comfort zones, they discovered that they could make their dreams a reality in ways they had never imagined. And it just so happens that they're all making a pretty decent living doing it, too.

You're also going to learn about some companies that are doing some of the most exciting things on the planet.

They're discovering ways to solve world hunger; they're working to make energy cleaner and more efficient; and they're developing the next wave of consumer technologies. Perhaps you too want to solve these problems, but never considered working for a company to do so. Again, it's time to expand your horizons a bit.

Some ideas I share with you may scare you and go against what you've been told about following your dreams. For instance, I want you to have a financially secure career, because financial distress is a dream killer that causes some of life's most difficult challenges. I'm not saying you need to be a millionaire; rather, I'm talking about earning a decent living *while following your dreams*. It can be done if you follow your dreams *in a smart way*.

Pursuing your dreams is important—you'll enjoy the forty or more years of your working life a lot more if you're doing something that interests you. But in order to truly succeed at your dreams, you need to ensure that you get the education and skills that will enable you to have a great career. Your dreams will be much easier to reach if you equip yourself with the problem-solving, critical-thinking, communication, and collaboration skills that are in high demand.

And that's what this book is for: to challenge you to realize your true potential as early as possible, to be smart about the dreams and goals you set for yourself, and to equip you to make decisions now that will set you up for future success.

TWO

Do You Have a Dream?

Not long ago, I stopped in a yogurt shop in Tampa. When I went to pay, I noticed there was a jar on the counter that read "Jacqueline's College Fund." I looked up at the young woman behind the counter and smiled, "You're Jacqueline?"

She nodded.

"Clever," I said, indicating the tip jar. "What are you studying in college?"

"I'm a psychology major," she said. "I'd like to be a psychologist."

"That's wonderful," I said. "Have you begun thinking about graduate school?"

I was just making friendly conversation and didn't intend to put Jacqueline on the spot, so her response surprised me.

"Why?" she asked. "Do I need to go to graduate school to become a psychologist?"

I was stunned. Even as a psych major, Jacqueline had never been told that she had to go to graduate school to become a psychologist. (While an associate's or bachelor's degree in psychology can equip you for a career in a host of fields, the American Psychological Association notes that "most state licensing boards of psychology require a doctoral degree to be a licensed therapist.") I spent the next few minutes helping Jacqueline understand what she had to do to become a psychologist. By the end of our talk, she was in tears.

"No one has ever told me this before," she said.

So many students enroll in college without any idea of what they want to do. That's a pretty expensive exploration process. Others go to college with some idea of what they want to do, but they haven't invested any time in discovering what a career in their chosen profession requires. That was Jacqueline's problem.

I want you to avoid those moments like the one Jacqueline had—"No one has ever told me this before" moments. So let's start minimizing those moments right now.

IF YOU'RE GOING TO FOLLOW YOUR DREAMS...

As I mentioned before, at some point in your life you probably have heard a famous person say something to the effect of "follow your dreams." If you haven't had to sit through a commencement address yet, just wait. The speaker will say something like "follow your passions," "be true to yourself," "trust your gut," or "this is the first day of the rest of your life."

All of those phrases actually appeared in commencement speeches delivered in recent years by high-profile speakers ranging from Ellen DeGeneres and Oprah Winfrey to Steve Jobs and Jim Carrey. I don't mean to criticize these celebrities—we could all learn something from their success. But the unfortunate reality is that the advice to "follow your dreams" has become a cliché—especially in commencement addresses.

There's nothing wrong with "following your dreams." It's a great rallying cry that's meant to inspire you, and it wouldn't be a cliché if there weren't some truth to it. Many writers and thinkers over the millennia have made the sentiment their own, including Henry David Thoreau: "If one advances confidently in the direction of his dreams, and endeavors to live the life which he has imagined, he will meet with a success unexpected in common hours…"

But being told to "follow your dreams" is too vague, so it doesn't really tell you what you need to know; it tells you what you want to hear. "So if I should just 'follow my dreams,' that means I don't really need to learn math, or science, or writing," goes the thinking for far too many young people. "Follow your dreams" glosses over the details. But details matter—*a lot.*

Better speakers will probably add "work hard" to the mix, lest you mistakenly think greatness and success will come easily if you just "follow your dreams." But, again, "work hard" and "follow your dreams" isn't a strategy for success because it doesn't help you find direction. You could work very hard at achieving your dream of becoming a VCR repair person—but good luck getting any customers.

So, let's be honest about this: "Follow your dreams" is a bit of graduation boilerplate that hides the real work ahead of you. It's rhetoric masquerading as a clarion call for greatness. It's not a plan; it's not even good advice. At most, it's just a reminder to avoid doing something you don't like.

Unfortunately, by pursuing your dreams without clear direction, you're far more likely to end up exactly where you don't want to be: doing something you don't enjoy. An article in *Psychology Today* aptly summed up many of the problems with the "follow your dreams" mentality. The author wrote:

> Another problem [with the exhortation to follow your dreams] is the assumption that anyone

can just drop everything they've built to follow an interest that may or may not be able to support them.... Unless your dream consists of working at a job that provides a healthcare [sic] and a living wage, most people with these longings can only really afford to indulge them in a part-time way. That's just life, and personal responsibility is arguably more valuable than any vague "passion."[1]

...FOLLOW THEM SMARTLY

None of this is to say that you should abandon your dreams. While it is important to receive "follow your dreams" advice with caution, it's just as important not to overcorrect. This can lead to cynicism, pessimism, self-doubt, and, ultimately, failure. Rather, you should pursue your dreams in the smartest way you can. This means taking your dreams out of the clouds and holding them up to the harsh light of day—doing a little introspection. Don't just hold your dreams close to your heart. Investigate them; try to understand them. Be able to answer the question, "Why do you want this?"

Many young people recoil from this type of internal investigation, and here's why. When a dream is still only a dream, it is without substance. It exists solely in the imaginer's mind; a sort of living daydream that he or she can recall at moments of trouble or self-doubt. In this idyllic existence, the dream encounters no obstacles, no resistance; there isn't an adult or authority figure to laugh at it, to tell you the dream is foolish, and to point you in a direction *they* feel you should go, which is decidedly the direction *you* don't want to take. Besides, once we start taking a hard look at our dreams, we might realize just how difficult it will be to achieve them.

FROM THE CLOUDS TO THE GROUND

Bringing your dream into reality doesn't have to be intimidating or disillusioning. Just imagine yourself in ten years. What are you doing? Be honest with yourself!

Ten years from now, I will be:

_____

Write in whatever your dream is—playing professional sports, working on a cure for cancer, inventing the technology that will replace the smartphone, helping people who are disadvantaged, writing a novel.

Have that dream in mind? Perfect, now I want you to list five things you need to do to make that dream a reality. Here, use this:

1.
2.

3.

4.

5.

How far did you get? If your dream is to become a doctor or lawyer, then I imagine you got pretty close to listing five things. Maybe if you want to be a doctor your list looked like this:

1. Get good grades in science courses.
2. Attend a good college or university with a strong pre-med program.
3. Prepare for and take Medical College Admissions Test (MCAT).
4. Attend a good medical school.
5. Doctor!

The educational and career pathways for doctors and lawyers are fairly linear. It's up to you to take the right courses and make good grades in high school and college, but after that, it's mostly a matter of whether you can persist through medical school and residency.

If you weren't able to come up with five steps, I suggest that part of the problem is that your "dream job" isn't very well defined, so you don't know how to get there. What is the path for someone who wants to be a scientist or an engineer or a writer?

This is actually a common problem. A recent survey by the networking site LinkedIn identified the top five childhood dream jobs of U.S. workers. For women, the top five childhood dream jobs were teacher, veterinarian, writer, medical professional, and singer. For men, they were professional athlete, pilot, scientist, lawyer, and astronaut.[2]

There's nothing outrageous about any of these dream jobs, but the LinkedIn list reveals a very common misconception among students about their future careers; those answers assume your "dream job" is a one-time thing. You get it, then it's yours forever. But that's not how a career works. This is similar to the problem you might have met if you didn't get very far on your list because your dream is more goal-oriented, rather than job-oriented. For example, what if you want to protect the environment? Or help reduce starvation? Or build the next generation PC? Assuming you had "go to college" written down somewhere on your list, what happens after that?

Don't worry if you didn't get very far. That's the point. It's unlikely that you know exactly what is required to fulfill your dream. Instead, you have this hazy vision of going to college, graduating, and then either quickly or slowly moving into your dream job. That's entirely normal. But it's also wrong.

Now, I'm in my dream career, but if you had asked me when I was seventeen how I could get here, I first would have told you that leading a STEM education organization sounded like the worst thing in the world. The second thing I would have said is that I had no clue how to end up there. My list would start and end with "Go to college."

Or perhaps you don't have much of a dream, in which case, you couldn't write down much of anything. That's also normal and not something that should concern you—yet. Even students with a firm idea about what they want to do with their lives may change their minds two, three, or even four times before they graduate from college.

According to the *Wall Street Journal*, "the median job tenure for workers aged 20 to 24 was shorter than 16 months. For those aged 25 to 34, it was three years, according to the Bureau of Labor Statistics, still far short of the 5.5-year median tenure for all workers aged 25 and older."[3]

We're going to get more into employment matters later, but for now this should tell you that you shouldn't look for a dream "job." What you're really looking for is a dream "career."

FROM "DREAM JOB" TO "DREAM CAREER"

Ideally your list should include steps on how to start out on the right career path. Getting a job isn't the end; it's one step of a journey. So, for example, you don't want to be a "scientist." You want to have a career in a specific scientific field. You don't want to be a "writer." You want to be able to make a living writing. This might seem like semantics, but stay with me.

Say your dream is to become a professional athlete. That's a job. Think bigger—perhaps something like, "I want to have a career in professional sports."

See the difference?

Let's take another "dream job." Instead of saying, "I want to be a singer," what about "I want to have a career in the music industry"? Looking at your dream in this way doesn't mean you can't be a professional soccer player or the next Lady Gaga. All it means is that you should stop looking at your dream as a single achievable goal and more as a lifelong pursuit.

Remember when I told you in the last chapter that your dreams could actually be limiting you? This is what I mean. Your focus on one job ignores all the other ways you can live your dreams besides that one job. When you change your focus from "professional athlete" to "career in professional sports," do you see how wide and promising your horizons can become?

By all means pursue athletics, but while you do so, start to think about all the other ways you can work in professional sports: sports medicine and science; management; coaching; marketing. Or take your love of singing. Do what you need to do to become a professional singer, but also look at how you might continue working in the music industry

that one job not materialize as you may
roducing; management; technology.

nefit of this exercise is to see if your pas-
cular industry extends beyond a specific
joa oes your love of sports extend beyond
you ? Does your love of music extend
bey ng? If your answer to questions
like t's time to think long and hard
about y ase you could risk spending the
bulk of y and post-college life in pursuit of a
single job t exclusion of all other possibilities, only
to realize that that one job will never be yours or that
you've missed better opportunities, because you were
thinking too narrowly.

Then what?

NO SUCH THING AS A PERFECT DREAM

We all prefer our dreams to remain in this unchallenged
state. But an unexamined dream is a dream that will never
become reality. As long you choose to protect your dream
from criticism, you will never move closer to living it. And
for some young people, this is all their dreams amount to.
Most people never have the courage to take their dreams
out of the sky and subject them to rational analysis. Why?
Because once your dream becomes a plan, then you're in
danger of failing.

They say most people's greatest fear is public speaking—sometimes maybe more than death—but I believe that it doesn't come close to our fear of failure. The fear of failure keeps our dreams in our heads, locked away, where they remain pristine and unspoiled. They also remain unrealized. If you want to achieve your dreams, you have to examine them, put them to the test, and have a plan for making them a reality. This book will show you how to put yourself on a path to success regardless of whether you have a dream. In fact, in the next chapter, I'm going to speak directly to those readers who don't have a dream.

But if you have a dream, then it's time to examine it. Let's bring it to the table, put it under the microscope, and see what we find. Just be forewarned: after we put your dream through the steps, it won't look the same. You might not even want to hang on to it after we're done. You're going to see holes and blind spots. It may not look as attractive or make as much sense as it used to. That's normal. And I think you'll be glad you saw those imperfections now rather than in five, ten, or fifteen years. Finding these flaws now frees you to find success with a new and better dream.

THREE

Beyond Your Wildest Dreams

Many of you weren't alive in 1989 when the movie *Dead Poets Society* hit theaters, but it provides a wonderful example for our discussion about dreams.

Set at an elite boarding school in the 1950s, the film relates how English teacher John Keating, played by the late, great Robin Williams, uses an unorthodox teaching style to inspire his students to become passionate about poetry. In one of the more exceptional scenes in the movie, Keating says to his students:

> We don't read and write poetry because it's cute.
> We read and write poetry because we are members

of the human race. And the human race is filled with passion. And medicine, law, business, engineering, these are noble pursuits and necessary to sustain life. But poetry, beauty, romance, love, these are what we stay alive for.

The backdrop to these moving lines is the school's rigid academic conformity. The students are taught their other courses, particularly what today we would call STEM courses, all by way of formulas and rote memorization. The students all have "dreams" of being doctors, lawyers, and engineers, although the audience knows that these are really their parents' dreams. Into this starched, dull world, Keating's teaching explodes like a lightning bolt, revealing a beauty behind education that the students never knew existed.

I mention this excellent film because the lessons Keating imparts to his students fit well with our discussion on dreams. How so? Well, let's turn the tables a bit. Let's suppose that the school Keating teaches at is actually one known for its dedication to the humanities, rather than STEM courses. Imagine that Keating is a math teacher whose students only care about poetry.

How would Keating reach them? How could he get them to see not only the beauty, but also the excitement, the "passion" behind mathematics? He might do it by talking about fighter jets in flight, sending a rocket ship to Mars, or cracking codes for the CIA. Jet engineer, rocket scientist, cryptologist—these are just some of the exciting ways mathematics is used outside the classroom. But too often the connection between the real world and STEM subjects such as advanced math is murky at best for middle or high school students. That's the fault of an educational system that focuses more on rote memorization than on learning STEM principles in relevant ways.

The way to appreciate poetry and literature is the same way to appreciate STEM subjects: understand how they apply to the real world. Sure, some students don't require creative teaching methods to get their hearts racing for Shakespeare or calculus, but many more do. Otherwise, it's just a bunch of squiggly lines in a textbook. Keating showed them the life behind poetry textbooks. That life exists behind the pages of a math, science, or physics book as well. The only question is whether you've been exposed to it.

I would never demean the importance of "poetry, beauty, romance, love." They *are* what we stay alive for. But, with apologies to a great movie, there is beauty in STEM too. There is also passion. These aren't just "noble pursuits and necessary to sustain life." Innovation is the engine of life. Innovation is making our world smarter, safer, and more efficient. Innovation is curing diseases, eradicating hunger, and developing new energy sources.

Innovation doesn't just put food on the table; it showcases the best of humanity—a team of minds coming together to solve a problem. You can be at the forefront of that innovation, that excitement, that passion—and you don't have to be exceptional at math.

DREAM BEYOND YOUR EXPECTATIONS

The students in *Dead Poets Society* didn't know they had a passion for poetry until Keating exposed them to it *in the right way*. Poetry was certainly part of the curriculum, just as mathematics was, but the way it was taught wasn't exactly inspiring. The school was simply checking a box, much like you're checking a box when you struggle through a course you dislike. Chemistry? Check. Algebra? Check.

I have no idea how well the STEM subjects are taught in your school. Maybe you love STEM because it's been taught in a relevant and engaging way, perhaps through a course designed by Project Lead The Way. Or maybe you love STEM in spite of how it's been taught to you. Perhaps you dislike it because of the way it's been taught.

What I can say for certain is that how you feel about STEM—or English or history—is a direct reflection of whether you think you're good at it. If you're bad at math, chances are good that you don't like it. Find writing difficult? Then you probably dislike English. That's just the way it works.

More importantly, if you're bad at math, *no one* is telling you to pursue a career in math. Your parents or teacher will do what they can—hire a tutor, for instance—so that you pass math, but that's just a way to improve your chances of getting into college. It's not really for the math itself. And so from a very young age, you have crossed off math from your list of "interests." Because you struggled with it early on, there was no one to help you see through the formulas and the equations to the beauty on the other side.

Have you ever thought of it like that? That your performance on a certain subject in school has *already* influenced your dreams and your career options? You've been told all your life that there isn't anything you can't do—except what you're not good at. If you're bad at algebra during your sophomore year in high school, it could ruin your desire to pursue a career that uses math.

Discouraging, isn't it? You may be just leaving high school and already doors are closing.

It's also completely wrong.

The truth is that most jobs that require math require *competence* at certain mathematical functions, not genius. So you're not Einstein with math—so what? As a jet engineer, you won't be asked to solve the mysteries of the universe. No one expects you to revolutionize the field of mathematics. You just need to know math well enough to build some awesome jets.

Look at it this way: say there's a marketing job out there that does a lot of business with Latin America. The employer will want whomever he hires to be fluent or competent in Spanish, given where his customers are. Is he looking for an applicant who was born and raised in Latin America and can speak Spanish as well as the natives? Sure, he'd love to have that applicant, just so long as that applicant can perform the actual job—marketing—as well as he speaks Spanish. But he'd most likely prefer a better marketer than a better Spanish speaker. Spanish is *a part* of the job; it's not the whole job or even half the job. You need to know it, but you don't need to have written books in Spanish.

Do you get the idea? I hope so, because we're going to return to it later.

Too often we stop pursuing things we're not especially talented at in favor of pursuing things that are more naturally easy for us. If you have a way with words and writing, you'd rather learn and study those subjects than bang your head against the wall studying physics.

But there's another reason we do it: that "follow your dreams" cliché. Parents, teachers, and counselors all give us the same advice—pursue your interests. For instance, if you demonstrate talent in music, you are encouraged to pursue music. If your history teacher sees that you're particularly good at understanding complicated historical lessons, she encourages you to pursue history. If you're sitting in your counselor's office wondering what to study in college, the first thing he's going to ask you is: "Well, what are you good at?"

In other words, there is a tremendous amount of pressure on you, from a very young age, to pursue only those endeavors, subjects, or hobbies that you're already good at. The older you get, the more attention you bring to these subjects and the less you have for those you may struggle with.

The school system, even in college, tries to make up for this by requiring a wide range of diverse course work. You have no choice but to take math, science, history, and English. That's just the way the system works. But within that system we all know that you're pushed toward focusing on the classes you prefer and simply passing on the ones you don't.

This pressure to pursue only the subjects you're good at has to have some effect on your dream. What I mean is that if you love English, it's unlikely you're going to want to be an electrical engineer. And if you love physics, it's unlikely you're going to pursue a career in communications. That's because you have no reason to ever look beyond your more obvious interests. Chances are no one is pushing you to think beyond your self-imposed limitations.

There's a serious problem here. If you dislike, say, physics, that probably has more to do with the school subject of physics than the practical application of physics in the real world. When you have the textbook open and you're trying to memorize the laws of thermodynamics, your brain shuts off and you wish you were anywhere else. But would your brain shut off during a rocket launch, when those same laws are working right before your eyes? I doubt it.

And yet, because you showed little aptitude for memorizing and understanding physical properties early on in your education, you were gently pulled away from any interest of pursuing physics as a career. You might love the possibilities of space exploration, but because you weren't initially "good at physics" you never really pursued that interest. Then one day, you're watching a documentary on rocket scientists and you think, "Now that looks like an exciting career." That's physics in the real world. My question: would you have gritted it out, pushed yourself a little harder, perhaps worked with a tutor, to get you through your rough patch of physics as a school subject, if it meant that one day you could be building rockets?

I hope you're beginning to understand that a lot of your dreams and your ambitions, while they might accurately reflect your true passions, are also the product of the way you've been pressured into focusing on certain subjects. The pressure doesn't just come from parents, teachers, or counselors, who really do have your best interests at heart, but also from self-imposed pressure—you do it to yourself. We all prefer the path of least resistance, but this preference doesn't come without some consequences.

You might wonder how I've come to this conclusion, and that's a fair question. I feel confident saying this because I see it every day. One of the greatest pleasures of my job is when I see a student like you finally *get* a subject that has tormented her for years. She didn't get it by keeping her nose in the books; she got it by *doing it*. My organization, Project Lead The Way (PLTW), makes sure that our students see how STEM subjects are applied in the real world. They see physics in action. They see electrical engineering in action. They see mathematics in action. In short, they see how STEM subjects are changing the world.

And most of them—not all—like what they see.

That's when the light comes on. When students see math and science principles in action, in a project they have led that involved critical thinking and problem solving, that's when the words in the textbook—those confusing, frustrating formulas and equations—suddenly leap off the page and come to life. They're the same words that had always troubled the student, but now she sees what they *really mean*. She sees that those words have power; that they are useful to achieve a certain task or solve a specific real-world problem.

Then physics or math or engineering aren't abstract concepts anymore—they're no longer just things we learn in case we become teachers one day. We learn them because we need them to do real, exciting things that expand our knowledge of the world; that propel humans to other worlds; that solve some of the most pressing problems right here on earth, such as hunger and disease, which have plagued humanity for thousands of years.

And they think: *I can do this*? It's a question at first, but then suddenly it's not. *I can do this*!

You can do it, too.

GOOD NEWS: YOU DON'T NEED TO BE GREAT

I hope you've already picked up on a theme here, but I'll put it plainly: you don't need to be great in a subject to pursue a career in that subject. You don't need to be a genius to be a pilot, astronaut, engineer, or rocket scientist. You have to be competent—and competent at some very high level math—but none of those careers are closed to you if you want them. The same is true for careers that require chemistry, physics, computer science, and engineering.

The same is true of the humanities, too. Do you know how many not great, but competent writers are making a lot of money and having a great career? I won't name names, but there are *a lot*. They learned the art of writing just well enough to become professional writers.

Likewise, to have a career in STEM you need to learn the STEM subjects just well enough. It's true that some careers require greater proficiency than others. I won't say that a C math student has the same chance as the A math student of becoming a rocket scientist. But here's what levels the playing field: do you want it bad enough? If the C student works harder than the A student, then she may level the playing field. Like much else in life, it often comes down to drive and desire.

GO FIND YOUR DREAM

One thing I don't want you to take away from this discussion is that I'm saying your passion or dream is wrong. Please don't read it that way. Rather, what I'm saying is that it's time to expand your horizons. It's time to break out from your comfortable world and dare yourself to imagine a *different dream.* What I want you to understand is how much your current dream or passion has been shaped by things really beyond your control. It might still be the right one for you, but don't you owe it to yourself to see if there's something else out there you might like even better?

In the next chapter I'm going to introduce you to a few former PLTW students who decided to pursue a career in STEM after taking our programs. I hope that their job experiences expose you to dreams and career paths you might not have considered.

FOUR

Dreams in Action

I t's time for me to step back for a moment and let you hear from others. I want you to meet three former students who are in the working world today. All of them pursued engineering in some way in college and as a career, although they all didn't end up in the same place. I hope you'll see some of the ideas and suggestions I presented in the last three chapters come alive in their stories.

THE MOMENT HE REALIZED HIS DREAM

Like a lot of young men, Quinn had vague dreams in junior high and early high school of becoming a professional athlete. He loved sports, particularly basketball, and figured it was the best path open to him.

"Unfortunately, I had two knee surgeries before the age of sixteen, which kind of wiped me out from pursuing that avenue," he told me. Although it's hard for any athlete to undergo those types of dream-ending injuries, it did force Quinn to look at what *else* he enjoyed. He was a good student, and especially strong in math and sciences. He also loved tinkering on cars, train sets, and whatever he could take apart and put back together in his garage. But that was his only exposure to any sort of engineering. His father was an entrepreneurial restaurant manager and his mother was a nurse—great jobs, but not exactly aligned with Quinn's interests. Speaking of what he does now, Quinn said, "I had no idea what it was."

It's certainly possible that Quinn eventually may have happened upon engineering, given his math and science talents. But aside from his meddling in the garage, there was nothing in his world that pushed him in that direction. That started to change when Quinn began taking Project Lead The Way courses in high school. As he told me:

> The first course that I took was "Intro to Engineering Design," which is pretty much the foundation course. You learn about the engineering design process: how you go from identifying a

problem to solving it. Then comes the actual designing, and then constructing your solution. *After that first course I knew this was something I wanted to continue with.* The program was fairly new and our class size was really small at that time. The next course I took was "Principles of Engineering," where you get deeper into theory: why things work, why they're designed a certain way, and how we can use them to solve even more problems.

After that second course, Quinn told me, "I started to notice a connection between some of the current course work that I was taking at the time, such as advanced algebra, geometry, and AP science, and my PLTW courses."

Quinn, a man now in his twenties, remembers this moment from high school when it all started to come together. "OK, this is why we study this; and this is why this works," he said. It's quite a moment for a young kid when the world starts making sense, when the things that seem irrelevant and beyond his capabilities suddenly become comprehensible.

Quinn told me about a time when he met some real-life electrical engineers during his PLTW course. One of them had gone to Quinn's high school and was now introducing Quinn and his peers to some engineers from the Institute of Electronics and Electrical Engineers (IEEE). The IEEE engineers let Quinn and his friends experiment with a Segway-type personal mover that they had built.

"They told us exactly how they came to design this and I realized I understood what they were saying," Quinn told me. "With the programming aspects, ordering parts, timeline, keeping schedule, all the things that we learned in our PLTW courses. It was at that moment that I was hooked. I said to myself, 'Electrical Engineering is what I want to do.'"

Today, Quinn is an electrical engineer at Chevron, a company he's worked for since college. Although he works in Houston, Quinn's main project is in Western Australia, where Chevron has a fairly large liquefied natural gas presence. And when I say "fairly large" I mean that Quinn, at twenty-six, is responsible for the electrical needs of a $200 million project. Not bad for a kid whose athletic dreams were cancelled by a couple of knee surgeries.

Here is Quinn's advice for you:

> When I go back home, the first thing I tell students is it's important to utilize all your resources, and take advantage of all opportunities. Teachers, parents, counselors, coaches—they don't want to see a student fail. I've never had the experience as a student where I've asked a question or asked for help where someone didn't step up and assist me.

Whether that's an after-school program, or a tutoring resource, those are the avenues that are available to students, but nine times out of ten the student won't raise their hand and say, "Hey, I don't get this." They would rather sit back and just let time pass, or say this really isn't for me. Don't shy away from the challenges. Don't worry if you're not good in math and science; it's something that you can work at if you put the time into it.

As a student, you never will have as much energy and passion as you do right now. When you're a student get involved in as many things as you can. Go out and learn what you're good at, learn what your weaknesses are, and then eventually build upon those weaknesses so you can become great at those things. Now is the time for you to see where you'll be in ten to fifteen years. You have to put in the work now so you can get where you want to be in the future.

A DREAM NEARLY THWARTED

When Mark goes to talk with a high school class, he usually has the same message: "When I was y'all's age, I was *not* good at math, terrible at it, bad." It isn't something the students expect to hear, given that Mark is an engineer for Lockheed Martin, one of the world's largest aerospace and defense companies.

Mark finds himself in front of high school students often as part of a Lockheed program called Engineers in the Classroom. As the name implies, real-life Lockheed engineers visit a classroom for a day, give a short talk, take students' questions, then conduct a hands-on demonstration. It's a great program, especially since it gives engineers like Mark—the self-professed bad math students—an opportunity to speak honestly with students.

But Mark's history as a bad math student is more than just a great line to deliver in front of a classroom. When I spoke with Mark, he emphasized his poor math skills again and again. Like many students who struggle with math, no one outside Mark's family encouraged him to pursue a math-related career. Unlike many students in his situation, however, Mark's family knew what he was capable of. He explained to me:

> I came from a family of engineers. My dad was an engineer; my granddad was an engineer; my great-granddad was an engineer; my uncle, my brother— all engineers. Everyone is an engineer, so it was never really a question of what I wanted to be. I always knew, and ever since I was old enough to

walk around with a bucket of nails I would help my dad out with stuff. So it was just always in my DNA. But it was also challenging because I was the only one in my family who just wasn't really gifted at math. I'm still not gifted! It just does not come naturally to me.

Mark got extra help on his math courses after school, but it was always a struggle. He even began to doubt not whether he *could* become an engineer; but whether he *wanted* to become an engineer. In other words, his poor math skills started to ruin Mark's dream of following the family trade. Then he discovered Project Lead The Way.

"It was the first time where you stop looking at equations," he told me. "You stop looking at graphs and charts, and you're actually looking [at] and touching engineering. That made all the difference." Although Mark didn't fully understand it at the time, he was a visual and kinesthetic learner—which means that he learned best when he put the book down and picked up the tools. It was only then that math started to make sense. Mark told me he was doing things in eighth grade as part of his PLTW courses that he does now as a Lockheed engineer. "My dad, who was an engineer, was like, 'What? You're doing what in class?'"

Aside from his improved math skills, Mark also felt his self-confidence return. He had all but given up on his engineering dreams, but now he knew he was meant for the family business. "I really felt like I was some type of engineer," he said. "It gave me a great sense of what it would be like twenty years down the road. In fact, some of the older guys I work with at Lockheed, they still don't know how to do some of the things I learned when I was in high school."

Of course, Mark still needed to make the grades to realize his engineering dreams. He might have known how the math connected to the engineering, but if he couldn't do the equations on the test, it wouldn't mean very much. The difference was that now he *knew* he was going to be an engineer. He *knew* exactly what kind and how much math was involved. And he *knew* he could do it. So when he had to return to the books, and the equations, and the tests, he did so with a rejuvenated spirit. Mark's passion pushed him to study math harder than anyone in his family had ever had to study for it. And it worked.

"Today, I'm about as good as any other engineer, but that's only because of brute force—hardcore studying every day," he told me. "No one made me go to tutoring, but I had to because I knew I needed it."

Mark graduated college in 2014 and immediately began work at Lockheed. His first job? He was a manufacturing engineer on the F-16 and F-22. The kid who wasn't good at math ended up working on two of the best fighter planes in the U.S. military arsenal. Now Mark is in Lockheed's Engineering

Leadership Development Program, an elite training course open to just twelve Lockheed engineers every year.

When we were talking over the phone, I could feel the excitement and passion in Mark's voice. So I asked him about it. Here's what he told me:

> If I had a free ticket to any job in the world, I would still have picked this particular role. It makes me wonder why everyone else in the world doesn't want to be an engineer. It's jaw-dropping to think that anyone would do anything else, but thank God that people do. You need to feel that way kind of about your job no matter what it is.
>
> Lockheed is definitely unique because it's hard not to be proud of our products. They're just kind of cool things. Even on my most boring day I sit a couple hundred feet from one of the jets, so I can go out there and check it out. Even as we're talking on the phone, I'm looking out over the flat line right now. I'm watching a bunch of planes fly around.

A DIFFERENT CALLING

Like Mark, Juliana knew she wanted to be an engineer from an early age. Unlike Mark, she was superb at math and her other courses.

"I was just very good at sort of playing the 'school game,'" she told me. "I knew what I had to do to get hundreds in my classes, and I was capable of doing it. I had the support at home from my parents to achieve my goals. I think I was just going through the motions because that's what you were supposed to do."

The ironic part is that Juliana is the only one you'll meet in this chapter who isn't a practicing engineer. She left GE to join the PLTW team.

In junior high and high school, Juliana knew she had a better grasp on her math and science courses than most of her peers. She never had much of a problem standing out in class. But when Juliana sat down with her guidance counselor, she was never told about practical courses like Project Lead The Way. Juliana found that odd, given that her father was a well-known civil engineer and that she was getting excellent grades in all her courses. But now she sees it a bit differently.

> There was really no reason they didn't tell me about the course besides that I was a girl. We talked about my interests in math and science, and even pursuing engineering, and I was in advanced classes in all those topics. So it really didn't make any sense that you wouldn't mention that to a student with the experience and interests that I had.

Sure, perhaps the guidance counselor simply overlooked PLTW courses. Maybe the guidance counselor saw a girl and mentally shut the "engineering" door because of stereotypes about "male jobs" and "female jobs."

It's unfortunate to think that this happens, but gender stereotypes likely lead to fewer girls pursuing engineering. *U.S. News and World Report* noted in 2016 that "Gaps between men and women...remained entrenched."[1] The same is true for gaps between white students and students of racial minorities. "As the number of white students who earned STEM degrees grew 15 percent in the last five years, the number of black students fell by roughly the same margin."[2]

Turning these numbers around will require a concentrated and intentional effort to provide girls and minority boys with access to relevant STEM opportunities, rather than dismiss STEM as something they aren't interested in or something that's too tough for them. But that's a subject for another book and, fortunately for Juliana, she knew she wanted to pursue engineering in spite of pressure to go another way. On the advice of a friend, she learned about PLTW. Juliana told me she took two PLTW courses her senior year and in one of them, a class of about twenty-five, she was one of only two girls. That's sad.

But Juliana looks back on it as a learning experience. "It was good preparation for what my college and professional experience would be as an engineer," she told me. "So it was actually really valuable to learn how to navigate a male-dominated field and not be intimidated or have it be a barrier, in any way, to my professional development."

Juliana also learned some more personal lessons in her PLTW courses. She already knew the academic work; and she discovered she was also very good (and passionate) about the practical engineering work. But it also gave her an unexpected lesson in what it means to lead:

> This was really my first experience, aside from athletics, of having some sort of leadership position. We had such a large project team, we broke up into smaller sub-teams that were working on different components of the project, and I was the group leader for one of those teams. I was the main person who had to communicate with professors at various institutions who would support our work. It was my first experience with any kind of leadership role in a more serious setting like that. It was a good way to learn how to share the work and not be overbearing. I had to learn how to lead that group in a successful way where everyone felt like a valued member of the team and there was accountability.

We rarely consider the more human side of fields like engineering, but in the working world, knowing how to lead a team is an immensely important skill. Engineers are used to being the smartest people in the room, and Juliana told me she was no exception. But her PLTW courses taught her something she didn't know she lacked. "It wasn't just about being the only girl; there was definitely some humility that needed to be learned," she told me.

After college, Juliana became an engineer at GE. During her two-year training program, she volunteered with Project Lead The Way to visit middle schools to discuss her engineering experience, particularly as one of the few females in the profession. Although Juliana wouldn't realize it until later, teaching suited her. She told me how she had always been fascinated with the way PLTW challenged even the best students.

"I saw the valedictorian get really frustrated in a PLTW course because there was no right answer," she told me. In other words, Juliana was able to grasp both the academic as well as the practical lessons of math and science. And she remembered the great mentors in her academic career who had a profound effect on her educational and personal success. At that point, forgoing a traditional engineering career in favor of teaching was the right path for her. And that's how Juliana ended up working at PLTW.

As with the other former students, I asked Juliana what sort of advice she had for you. Here's her reply:

I think two things. One would be, find other people who have similar dreams as yours and learn together about what that path is and what makes sense. I would also say find a mentor. That was something that was hugely impactful to me. One of my PLTW teachers in high school was a huge mentor during that time in my life, and continues to be a great friend.

Having mentors helps you understand two things. One, who you are, or at least, what you really want in life, and then how you can get there. Both the people who have been my mentors were involved with education and with STEM, so they helped on both sides of the fence there.

I would say find peers who can be peer mentors and who you can collaborate with and sort of learn from your collective experiences. You want mentors who can encourage your dreams and your passion, but in a reasonable way, not to knock people down at all, but to make sure that you are still able to support yourself.

I see that with people I know. I mentor and advise college students currently and I see students who, similar to me, were really, really good at playing the school game and following the prescribed path. Then you get to a point where there is no prescribed path and that's very confusing and then they realize, "I've never actually thought about this. I've just followed the prescribed path most of my life." That's when a mentor is most valuable.

We'll be hearing again from Quinn, Mark, and Juliana later in the book. For now, I hope you've gained a little bit of insight into your own dreams so you can look at them from a slightly different perspective. Perhaps they haven't changed at all; and perhaps they have changed radically. Or maybe you have no idea what your dreams are now! In whatever state you find your dreams, remember that as long as you analyze your dreams honestly and smartly, then you'll be able to answer the question I posed at the beginning of this section in the right way.

So: *what is your dream?*

FIVE

The World Doesn't Care About Your Dreams

Most people don't like talking about money. It's an annoying conversation in the best of circumstances, and humiliating in the worst. So it's unlikely that a commencement speaker will bring up planning for future financial well-being. It's often assumed in their advice about "following your dreams" that the money will come, magically. It's implied that if you work hard and go confidently "in the direction of your dreams," as Thoreau says, that you will eventually make enough money to be happy.

There's no other way to say it: this isn't true.

The true cost of the "follow your dreams" cliché is playing out in homes across the United States, as more and more college graduates go back to living with mom and dad after they've graduated because they can't support themselves. It's not unusual for students to lean on family for financial support during their college years, whether for tuition or living expenses, but around half say they expect to still need financial assistance from their parents *after* they graduate.[1] The polling company Gallup found that 28 percent of U.S. adults aged twenty-four to thirty-four who live at home are college graduates.[2]

Accepting financial assistance from your parents isn't a mark of failure, either personally or professionally. Some graduates undoubtedly do it despite having a good job that could pay the bills. They figure that if they can save a bit of money, why wouldn't they? More power to them, so long as there is an end point.

But many more who are financially dependent on their parents are not there by choice. They didn't make a conscious decision to rely on mom and dad for support, but they find themselves having completed college without acquiring the skills they need to pursue their dreams.

Make no mistake, financial distress is a dream killer and brings many of life's hardest challenges. The good news is that a little bit of smart planning can insulate you from one of the biggest obstacles to financial independence and realizing your dreams.

THE COST OF LIVING ON YOUR OWN

Before you can decide whether the education and career path you're starting down will earn you enough money to live comfortably, you have to define what it means to live comfortably. Your definition of comfort will undoubtedly be different from mine, but here are a few baseline characteristics as a starting point:

1. You're making more than you're spending.
2. You can afford basic necessities (food, clothing, shelter) and utilities.
3. You can make your charitable contributions.
4. You have a little left over to either save or spend on hobbies and other activities. (Hint: Save, save, save.)

In this exercise it's helpful to have a general idea of what those "basic necessities" will cost. The Economic Policy Institute's Family Budget Calculator tabulates average living expenses—housing, food, and health care—in U.S. cities. Here are a few:

- New York, NY: $46,519
- Boston, MA: $42,358
- Washington, DC: $45,119
- Atlanta, GA: $34,303
- Dallas, TX: $30,617
- Chicago, IL: $34,334
- Denver, CO: $31,829
- Los Angeles, CA: $37,886
- San Francisco, CA: $46,581

These are most certainly *estimates*. Why do I stress that? Because EPI's calculator uses a monthly housing expense (rent) of $1,191 in San Francisco. If you can get a one-bedroom apartment in San Francisco at that price in a safe neighborhood, I want to know your broker. Last year, the *San Francisco Chronicle* reported that the average monthly rent for a one-bedroom apartment in the city was $3,500.[3]

For New York, EPI estimates monthly housing costs at $1,163, even though the average rent in 2015 for a studio apartment in Manhattan was $2,351.

You should expect similar discrepancies in housing costs between the EPI estimates and averages reported elsewhere for all the major cities listed. To be on the safe side, I'd add two to three thousand more dollars per month to EPI's estimates, not just to account for housing realities, but also to give you some buffer.

I should also tell you that I added $3,000 to EPI's number for each city. Why? Because the average monthly student loan payment is $250—or $3,000 a year. If you don't expect to have student loan debt, knock off that $3,000 and thank your parents or your own hard work in getting a scholarship or paying your own way. For the rest of you, however, keep that $3,000 right where it is.

I probably don't need to stress the point, but here it is: you *must* know how much it costs to live comfortably before you decide what you will do with your life beyond college.

If you miscalculate—or, worse, don't calculate at all—you will find yourself in a terrible hole very quickly. Even if EPI's yearly expenses in America's major cities are slightly lower than they should be, they nevertheless give you a good idea of what to expect.

Once you know how much it's going to cost to live where you want or expect to live, you can get a general idea of how much you can expect to earn based on your major. The National Association of Colleges and Employers has calculated the average salaries for recent college graduates based on their majors. Here are a few:

- Business: $49,035
- Computer science: $69,214
- Engineering: $63,764
- Mathematics and statistics: $58,553
- Social sciences: $40,964
- History: $38,936
- Visual and performing arts: $38,470
- English: $38,125[4]

It doesn't take a genius to see which majors give you a better shot at living comfortably, nor should it come as a surprise. None of this is a reason to give up your dreams for a career in the humanities, but you should go in with your eyes wide open. Don't be blindsided by what the world pays employees with those majors or by the cost of living in certain cities.

As you progress through college, keep an eye on the living costs of your favorite cities as well as the average salaries of your chosen major. If you do this, you will be ahead of your peers. You won't be surprised by the high cost of living in America's major metropolitan centers or by the salary on your first offer letter. The lifestyle you see on TV—with young twenty-somethings living in spacious apartments, spending freely on going out with their friends—is in fact rare.

Two factors will lead you into a financial ditch very quickly if you're not careful: student loans and unemployment. Let's get to those now.

AMERICA'S STUDENT LOAN CRISIS

Much of the current political discussion about student loans has very little to do with you, at least right now. The rising costs of college, and the necessity for students to take out bigger and bigger loans, is untenable in the long run. Something will have to give, eventually.

But let's focus on the more immediate question of how this affects *you*. As I'm sure you already know, college is very expensive and growing more so every year. According to the National Center for Education Statistics, the average tuition (which includes fees, room, and board rates), charged for full-time undergraduate students of a four-year institution in 1982 was $10,385. In 2013, it was $23,872. For public four-year institutions, the average tuition in 1982 was $7,534. In 2013, it was $17,474. Finally, the average tuition of a four-year private institution in 1982 was $16,797. Thirty years later, the cost has grown to $35,074.[5] The numbers vary depending on what is included in the total cost, but you get the picture.

You would think that there is a ceiling that would halt costs. After all, eventually people won't be able to afford it, right? Well, the College Board estimates that the average tuition increase for a four-year public institution right now is 3.4 percent. For private schools, it's 2.4 percent. Although these are actually better than they've been in the past, the point is that any prices I present to you now will be outdated in a couple years. At the moment, the cost is still rising.

How can students' families keep paying for this? The answer for many is student loans, which are right now open to just about anyone who wants to go to college. Easy access to money comes with consequences. In 2012, the average debt for all graduating seniors with student loans was $29,400, a 25 percent increase from 2008. In 1993, for instance, the average debt was $9,450, when 47 percent of students graduated with loans. In 1996, this figure rose to 59 percent; 64 percent in 2000; 68 percent in 2008; and 71 percent in 2012.[6]

In 2014, the total debt owed by Americans who have student loans was $1.2 trillion, an 84 percent jump since 2008. Some 40 million Americans now have student loan debt, 11 million more than in 2008.[7] Unless you have access to other resources or earn a scholarship, you will join your fellow Americans in owing a good deal of debt after graduation.

Now, perhaps you've heard political discussions about cancelling all student loan debt or making college free. Don't count on either one of those ideas to become reality, especially not before you're ready to go to college.

Rather, look at student loans as an incentive. What do I mean by that? First, there's a growing trend among undergraduates to extend their college years beyond the traditional four years. In my day, we used to joke about fellow students who were on a "five-year plan" because they weren't smart or committed enough to finish in four years. It's not a joke anymore. Your parents might be surprised to know that it now takes college students an average of six years to complete a bachelor's degree.[8]

This is a bad idea for many reasons, but the biggest is that the longer you stay in college, delaying your entry into the job market, the more debt you will accumulate. How much more debt each year? Perhaps $23,000 for every extra year.[9] Combined with other school-related expenses and potentially $50,000 per year in lost earnings, that's a net loss of approximately $150,000 to stay in school.

It's hard to explain debt's crippling nature. Yes, holding a moderate and manageable level of debt is just fine and doesn't hurt your credit in the least. But holding no debt is better. Debt payments must be made or very bad things happen. You can't just get rid of it. Declaring bankruptcy doesn't make your student loan debt go away. So read carefully and understand this: you *must* make your student loan payments. Here's a brief overview of what would happen to you if you failed to do so several times in a row, what's otherwise known as "defaulting" on your loan.

- Wage garnishment: Your lender, either the federal government or a private bank, could start deducting a specific percentage from your paycheck. In most cases, what the lender is taking out of your paycheck will be more than your original student loan payment. Why? Because once you default, then additional costs start piling on, from higher interest rates to collection fees. You will *always* end up paying more in default than before.

- Lowered credit score: When you default on your student loan payments, the lender notifies the three national credit bureaus, which will include the default on all your future credit reports. Even if you resolve your default, the derogatory mark on your credit report could follow you for years and affect your ability to purchase insurance, get a credit card, a car loan, or a mortgage. It may even affect your ability to get a job.

- Legal troubles: Once in default, the lender can also sue you. You don't want to get sued.

What makes all this even worse is that this is all public information. What this means is that anyone who's interested—such as a future employer—can discover your legal history. So even after you've resolved the default, it stays with you, sometimes forever.

An all-too-real scenario is the story of the liberal arts major who attends graduate school to receive a master's in fine arts or creative writing. This student already took out loans for his four years as an undergraduate. He will take out another loan for at least two more years. And yet when he's finally finished, he's accumulated a large amount of debt and discovers that the salary base for a Master of Fine Arts degree with one year of experience is $43,000.[10] He probably owes twice that in student loans. This is not a recipe for comfortable living after college; it's a recipe for disaster.

So I say again: don't get blindsided by student loans!

Student loan debt is an unfortunate reality in today's university landscape. While it allows so many more people to attend college who otherwise couldn't afford it, student loan debt immediately puts one in a financial hole after graduation. That's not necessarily a bad thing. As I said, it could be an incentive to work harder in school so that you have your choice of jobs after graduation. It could be an incentive for you to keep going after that first elusive job after dozens of rejection letters. But if you don't have control of your debt, it will overwhelm you.

IT'S NOT EASY OUT THERE

While we're confronting harsh realities of life after college, let's dispense with another myth. The idea that just obtaining your college degree guarantees you a job might have been true in the past. It isn't any longer.

In fact, the unemployment rate for recent college graduates is at historic highs. There are several reasons for this, some of which we'll get into later. For now, let's just examine the extent of the problem so you know what's waiting for you.

In tracking four groups of prospective employees—college graduates, recent college graduates, young workers of college age but without a degree, and all workforce-age people—a Federal Reserve of New York study found college graduates experience about half the unemployment rate of all workers. This demonstrates the value of a college degree if nothing else. But the Federal Reserve also found that, "for recent college graduates, unemployment was consistently higher than for college graduates as a whole."[11]

One recent study put the "recent college graduate" unemployment rate at almost 9 percent, with an "underemployment" rate of nearly 17 percent.[12]

Underemployment describes those workers who are working part-time when they want full-time employment, or who have jobs beneath their education level—such as an MBA graduate working in a non-management job at McDonald's. She is employed in a strict sense, but would count as "underemployed." Regardless, unemployment and underemployment are much higher than they have been over the past twenty years or so—it's not something your older siblings or those who will be your bosses and managers in the workforce faced.

Unemployment and underemployment for recent college graduates is not a particularly new phenomenon. After all, it can take time to break into the job market, especially when the overall economy is down or in a sluggish recovery. What is new, according to the Federal Reserve's research, is that recent graduates "are increasingly working in low-wage jobs or working part-time ... [and] that while elevated rates of unemployment and underemployment may be typical for recent college graduates, finding a good job has indeed become more difficult."

The rates of highest unemployment for recent college graduates are in the fields of the liberal arts and the social sciences—indeed, the unemployment rates in those areas are three and four percentage points higher than for graduates in math and engineering. As the Federal Reserve concluded, "those who choose majors that provide technical training, such as engineering or math and computers, or majors that are geared toward growing parts of the economy, such as education and health, have tended to do relatively well." On the flip side, those "at the other end of the spectrum," with majors in subjects like communications and social sciences, "have not tended to fare particularly well in recent years."

The point is that it's hard out there for recent college graduates. You can certainly find work, particularly with the rise of the "sharing economy." Services like Uber and TaskRabbit allow anyone to earn a few more bucks, but these are not long-term solutions. And yet those student loan payments keep coming. The lender doesn't care if you're having problems with finding degree-appropriate work or if your salary is lower than you thought it would be. You must pay. You must always pay.

I know that this chapter has been a bit of a downer, but it's important for you to understand in crystal clear detail what's waiting for you after college. This is the unfortunate reality for far too many young adults.

Their fate doesn't have to be your fate. You can live comfortably after college, pay off your student loan, and have a little bit extra for fun and savings. But you need to know what you're getting into. Remember the second question I posed in chapter one: *will you be ready for this rapidly evolving world?*

This chapter has been an attempt to open your eyes to some financial realities. Now it's time to learn more about what kind of world you'll be facing when you graduate.

SIX

It's Not Your Parents' Economy

Y ou've probably heard about driverless cars. They're also known as autonomous vehicles, and they promise to revolutionize the way human beings travel.

In any given year, roughly thirty thousand Americans die from motor-vehicle accidents.[1] In countries such as China and India, where road fatality records are not nearly as comprehensive as in the U.S., estimates put the death toll in the hundreds of thousands of people every year.[2]

Of course, nearly all accidents on the road are caused by human error. The promise and hope of driverless cars is that once the element of human error is removed, our roads will become significantly safer. Whether we're talking about reducing automobile fatalities by 50 percent, 75 percent, or perhaps even 95 percent, the impact will be massive. Thousands of lives around the globe will be saved every year. Maybe traffic accidents will be something you tell your grandchildren about as a thing of the past.

Because of this, major automobile manufacturers are working on their own versions of autonomous vehicles. In most cases, we've seen the result of their work in small, but remarkable new features such as automated parallel parking and motion sensors that make the car avoid danger on its own. There are other features you've probably seen, such as GPS navigation, that have turned the dashboard into a computer.

The inside of today's car doesn't just look like a computer; the car itself has become a computer. Just like your smartphone collects reams of data about you and your environment, today's cars are constantly collecting data on everything from the speed you drive to how often you change your oil. Car companies use this data to make cars safer and more efficient. They want to learn all they can about how we drive, how the car operates, and what conditions lead to accidents. This information will help them build a better car tomorrow, then improve even on that one.

What this means, though, is that today's automobile manufacturers are also tech companies. Ford, Chrysler, General Motors—the titans of America's automotive sector for the last sixty years—are not all that different than the companies in Silicon Valley. Yes, cars are still made in massive, assembly-line factories much as they've always been, but so are iPhones and laptops. Yes, the primary machine on a car is the combustion engine, a piece of technology that is anything but cutting edge. But the newer models, especially the hybrids and electric cars, use engines that are smaller, cleaner, and operate more like computer processors than traditional engines. The loud, dirty, and inefficient combustion engine will become a museum relic probably in your lifetime.

But what is the surest sign that automobile manufacturers are also tech companies? Google is building cars. By some accounts, Google is leading the race to build the first fully autonomous car—and that alone should tell you everything you need to know about the economy you will enter after you graduate from college. Because of technology, many major industries are slowly but steadily converging. Ford looks more and more like Google and Google looks more and more like Ford.

So what is happening to the world economy? In a word, transformation. The days of clearly delineated industries and careers are fast becoming a thing of the past. There was a time when the only type of engineer who would work at Ford was someone who knew everything about combustion engines. But now Ford needs electrical engineers, programmers, and data analysts. These are the very same people who are also highly sought after by companies like Google, Facebook, and Uber. Likewise, Google needs engineers who know about car manufacturing. Lines are now blurred. Career paths are anything but linear.

I'm focusing on the automobile industry because it's a great example of the type of technological convergence that is transforming our economy. But the transformation is all around us. In some way, every company is a tech company today. Every company needs employees who know how to code, program, and innovate. From publishing to cars to furniture manufacturers, no industry on this planet functions without vast reams of engineering skill, computer science, and data analytics.

What does this mean for you, someone who has grown up with this technological revolution? Everything.

No matter what your dream is, it's likely you're fairly competent in the use of your personal gadgets. I'm referring to your smartphone, computer, and other devices that are part of everyday life. Believe it or not, knowing how to use these things used to set people apart in the job market. Now, nearly every job out there assumes a degree of technical proficiency that even non–college graduates possess.

But that means that to stand out in today's economy you need to know more than how to tweet and text from your smartphone. What makes this economy—*your* economy—different than the economy your parents entered as college graduates? What are its main features? Its unique challenges?

This topic is far too big to cover in a single chapter. So right now we're going to look at three features of this new economy to help you understand what's going on out there.

DATA, DATA, DATA!

We're going to start this overview of today's economy by talking about something that has come of age exclusively with your generation. I'm talking about digital data, a term that refers to all the information that is created by our use of digital devices.

For instance, every time you tweet or Instagram, you've created digital data. Every time you send an email, you've created data. Your smartphone right now is creating data—reams of data, which is amazing. What's even more amazing is that 90 percent of the world's data was generated over the span of two years.[3] As Shawn DuBravac notes in his book, *Digital Destiny: How the New Age of Data Will Transform the Way We Work, Live, and Communicate*, every second, over 205,000 new gigabytes are created—or 150 million books' worth. DuBravac reports on the results of a study from the research firm IDC:

Forget the puny exabyte; we're on *zettabytes*—
that's 10^{21} or 1 *sextillion* bytes. In 2013, the IDC
report calculated that the world created 4.4
zettabytes of data. As the report notes by way of
comparison, if the digital universe were repre-
sented by the memory in a stack of PC tablets, in
2013 the stack would have "stretched two-thirds
of the way to the Moon." What's more, the digital
universe *doubles in size* every two years—eat your
heart out, Gordon Moore. By 2020, the data we
create and copy annually will reach 44
zettabytes—enough data to create 6.6 stacks of
PC tablets to the moon.[4]

This report came out several years ago, which means
that the digital universe has doubled in size yet again. We
pretty much know the reason. The explosion of personal
computing in the last quarter of the twentieth century, com-
bined with the spectacular rise of the Internet, launched the
new economy in the 1990s. For example, 1995 saw the start
of Yahoo!, eBay, and Amazon; the first web browsers,
Netscape Navigator and Internet Explorer; and Disney's
release of the movie *Toy Story*, the first completely com-
puter-generated movie.

You've never known a world that didn't have the Internet, but consider this: the world economy has changed more

between your parents' generation and your generation than anything we've seen since the invention of electricity. Think about that for a moment. The considerations, problems, and solutions with which your parents had to contend when they were your age are from another world. Yes, some problems and lessons are universal and don't change. But so many of the skills necessary to compete and thrive in today's economy weren't important when your parents were in school.

It took about thirty years for the refrigerator to become a staple in every U.S. home, according to the Harvard Business Review.[5] It took nearly sixty years for 100 percent of U.S. homes to have electricity. Other older technologies like the telephone and clothes washer likewise became commonplace over several decades.

Compare those slow rates of adoption to the cell phone, which took only ten years to reach 90 percent of U.S. homes. That's an astonishing rate of adoption, and it's only getting faster.Take the smartphone, probably the most important piece of technology you own. The smartphone is the fastest adoption by U.S. households since television. And we don't just see this in the United States. As a Harvard researcher notes, in 2001 the developed world had six times as many mobile subscriptions per capita as the developing world. By 2011, the gap had shrunk to 50 percent more phones per capita. "Of the world's six billion mobile-phone subscriptions, 73 percent are now in the developing world, even though those countries account for just 20 percent of the world's GDP," writes the Harvard researcher.[6]

Much like the immensity of our own physical universe, the effect this explosion of data has had on the economy is hard to appreciate. Yet one thing is certain: the digital data revolution has fundamentally transformed the way the economy works. In turn, this has affected how companies operate, which, lastly, has affected the type of skills an employee needs to compete in this new world.

Which also means that in two years, when the amount of digital data has doubled in size yet again, the economy will look different than it does today. How in the world can anyone hope to keep up? The simple answer is that a lot of companies and workers aren't keeping up at all.

THE GREAT DESTRUCTION

The reality is that all this transformation has led to some unfortunate consequences. Economists refer to this issue as "creative destruction," by which they mean that innovation and newer technologies render older technologies obsolete. For example, have you ever used a typewriter? Thirty years ago, typewriters were more common than computers. No one uses them anymore. An entire industry, one that had been around for more than a hundred years, is gone completely. Vanished!

But does anyone miss the typewriter? Is our world worse off because no one uses a typewriter anymore? Not at all. No one would trade his PC for a typewriter. That's creative destruction. Of course, it's not just typewriters. The most recent and telling example of creative destruction is the stunning rise of the ride-sharing company Uber. Founded in San Francisco in 2009, Uber now operates in nearly sixty countries and about three hundred cities worldwide.[7] Uber has thrown the global taxi-cab industry into chaos. I have no doubt you've been in a traditional taxi, but your children probably will never have to "hail" one on the side of the road.

It's not that the taxi companies couldn't have used the same technology that Uber uses. But they thought that their industry was safe. They didn't see the need to change, to adopt the newer technologies, because there was no reason to. Then Uber came along, and suddenly there was a reason to change with the times. That's the thing about this new economy you're about to enter: it loathes stagnation. From the beginning of history, companies have had to adapt to newer technologies and different customer demands. That hasn't changed. What's changed is how quickly this happens today.

The surge of data and transformational technologies has forced companies to become less resistant to change. They must change if they want to survive. But to do that they need employees who appreciate the importance of moving forward. They need employees who appreciate how the explosion of digital data has forever transformed the life-cycle of businesses.

A LACK OF SKILLED WORKERS

The final factor of this new economy is more or less a result of the first two. Namely, it's not just companies that struggle to keep up with the tremendous rate of change; it's workers as well. There's mounting evidence that the skills needed by the emerging workforce to compete in this new economy aren't necessarily the skills that most college graduates possess.

Some people think that this is the perfect time to be an entrepreneur running your own start-up. While today's entrepreneurs have vastly more power at their fingertips than ever before, the idea that it's consequently easier than ever to build a company from scratch is mostly fantasy. A 2014 article in the *Wall Street Journal* noted that the "creation rate of new businesses, as well as new plants built by existing firms, was about 30% lower in 2011 (the most recent year of data) compared with the annual average rate for the 1980s."[8] The article goes on to say that worker productivity in the U.S. is at historic lows as well. "[B]usiness output is nearly $1 trillion less today than what it would be had productivity continued to grow at its average rate of about 2.5% per year," the article reports. One reason for this, the article reports, is "that entrepreneurs report being hamstrung by difficulties in finding skilled workers."[9]

It's a common complaint among many business owners:

> Even students who graduate from the nation's elite universities often lack basic workplace skills, according to many of our participants.... In addition to general education deficiencies, we frequently heard the more specific problem of a severe national shortage of graduates with backgrounds in science, technology, engineering, and mathematics...[10]

This comes from the 2013 book *Where the Jobs Are: Entrepreneurship and the Soul of the American Economy* by John Dearie and Courtney Geduldig. The authors traveled the country talking to small business owners and entrepreneurs to understand some realities in this new economy. They were a bit surprised by what they saw:

> The most startling message we heard from entrepreneurs at our roundtables was that the most serious obstacle to additional hiring by new businesses is a pronounced shortage of qualified

talent. With 24 million Americans either unemployed or underemployed, we did not expect to
hear about a labor shortage...[11]

What follows is just a little taste of what some business
leaders told the authors:

> We're in the fortunate situation when we're expe-
> riencing a lot of growth—the company's doubled
> in size in six months...The biggest concern I have
> from a hiring perspective is getting talent in this
> town [Austin, TX]...I have the jobs, I just don't
> have the talent to fill them. We're really all fighting
> over the same talent.

> They go to schools that we're all familiar with
> that are supposed to be producing great tal-
> ent...But in terms of being useful on day one,
> they're just not. There's not enough focus on the
> fundamentals that ultimately make you useful and
> productive on day one.

> Companies want real life, hands-on experi-
> ence...but they're saying they'll get an engineer
> from a great university with a great GPA, and
> great knowledge about how to design and create

a particular part—but they don't know how to turn the machine on. They have no real-world application of how to actually get that part through the production process.[12]

A 2015 study from the Association of American Colleges and Universities (AACU) also found evidence supporting this idea that recent college graduates aren't ready for the new economy.[13] The report says:

> When it comes to the types of skills and knowledge that employers feel are most important to workplace success, large majorities of employers do NOT feel that recent college graduates are well prepared. This is particularly the case for applying knowledge and skills in real-world settings, critical thinking skills, and written and oral communication skills—areas in which fewer than three in 10 employers think that recent college graduates are well prepared. Yet even in the areas of ethical decision-making and working with others in teams, many employers do not give graduates high marks.

Notice that very little of the concerns expressed by these employers has anything to do with STEM education.

Rather, these are skills that have become important in the wake of the economic transformation spurred by the rise of digital data. Of course, some of these skills were important in prior generations as well, but many of them, such as "analyzing/solving complex problems," can't so much be taught in a book as they are learned from experience. In any job market, there have always been certain fundamental skills that one must possess to compete and succeed. And yet many of those fundamentals have changed from when your parents were your age. The problem is that the change has occurred so swiftly, mirroring the spectacular adoption rate of newer technologies, that many students have been left behind.

THE BEST OF TIMES, THE WORST OF TIMES

In many ways, this is the most exciting time to be young and in school, preparing for your career. The possibilities are nearly endless as far as where you can work and what you can achieve. No longer does an engineer or a mathematician have to work for a huge manufacturing company. They can just as easily work in Silicon Valley. No longer does a coder need to work for the same tech start-up where all his friends work: he can work in Detroit and design tomorrow's autonomous cars. The new economy allows for this because, much like the tributaries of a river, all industries are converging into one. That's a bit of an overstatement, but only a little. The point is that the skills you possess and acquire through education and experience can be used in many ways.

But of course there's bad news too. As I indicated above, employers are having a hard time finding new employees with the skills required to do these new types of jobs. How does one know if they possess these new, high demand skills? If colleges are failing to teach them, then how can one learn them? Don't worry, we're going to get to that soon.

SEVEN

Where to Find Jobs

A s you think more about the evolving economy and your place in it, it's important to have a good idea of where the jobs are, in terms of both fields of work and geographic locations.

Consider this for a moment: despite the nearly two million college graduates put into the field every year, the U.S. still needs to import some eighty-five thousand foreign workers to fill our needs in the areas ranging from science to engineering. This means the U.S. education system simply doesn't produce enough graduates with the skills employers need.

If you want to stand out in this new economy, look at what this country needs to import. No country, as a rule, imports what it doesn't need or already has.

A recent report from the Brookings Institution found that "20 percent of all jobs require a high level of knowledge in any one STEM field. STEM jobs have doubled as a share of all jobs since the Industrial Revolution, from less than 10 percent in 1850 to 20 percent in 2010."[1]

Even more recently, Brookings reported: "[J]ob openings data provide new evidence that, post-recession, STEM skills, particularly those associated with high levels of educational attainment, are in high demand among employers. Meanwhile, job seekers possessing neither STEM knowledge nor higher education face extraordinary levels of competition for a scarce number of jobs."[2]

The Government Accountability Office recently reported a related stat: "Both the number of science, technology, engineering, and mathematics (STEM) degrees awarded *and the number of jobs* in STEM fields increased in recent years [emphasis added]. Since 2004, the number of STEM jobs increased 16 percent from 14.2 million to 16.5 million jobs in 2012, and non-STEM jobs remained fairly steady."[3] In other words—there is growth in employment in STEM fields, whereas growth elsewhere is on a flat line.

According to yet another report issued by the education think tank Change the Equation and reported in *Scientific American*, "unemployed people outnumbered job postings by well more than 3-to-1."[4] However: "Across the STEM fields, job postings outnumbered unemployed people by almost 2-1."[5]

And as my organization, Project Lead The Way, reports: "The U.S. Department of Commerce estimates 1.2 million unfilled STEM jobs by 2018 as a result of a lack of qualified, trained workers. Coincidentally, STEM jobs are expected to grow by 17 percent, nearly double the rate of jobs in other sectors."[6]

You probably get the point by now. There's no getting around a simple fact: if you want to improve your employment chances as well as your earning potential, a career in STEM is one of your best options. Although there are few guarantees in life, you can increase your odds for success. STEM is a very good decision if you are interested in maximizing your opportunities at employment after high school and college.

Former U.S. Secretary of Education William Bennett is a friend and colleague of mine. Two years ago, he wrote a book—*Is College Worth It?*—questioning the economic value of going to college. Though he and I agree on many things, the central premise of his book was one we disagreed on. At the end of the day, I think the data bear out the value of a college degree both in the immediate and long term—unemployment rates, for college graduates, are less than half that for those with just a high school diploma.[7]

But Dr. Bennett had a line in his book I will never forget, and one we absolutely agree upon: "If you are accepted into the Colorado School of Mines, Harvey Mudd, Stanford, Plan II at the University of Texas, and dozens of other places...then go. And if you want to study petroleum engineering or any kind of engineering and have an aptitude for it, then go."[8]

What were Dr. Bennett and his co-author, David Wilezol, saying? No matter the debate about liberal arts education and its value, there is no debate about the value of higher education and STEM. We can debate liberal arts— but the consensus among those who disagree about the state of higher education and its general value is: STEM education is simply and unarguably valuable.

BUILDING A STEM FOUNDATION

Before I get to some more of this data, let's discuss the unpredictable. If there is one good reason to have a solid base of an education, it may be the foundation it gives you to be prepared for changing markets and times. Someone who went into telecommunications twenty years ago did so about eleven years before there was even such a thing as an iPhone. The idea that we could use our regular-sized watches as telephones was almost an impossible thought outside of a James Bond movie or a cartoon. Now, as we know, you can do more than take or place a phone call on your watch—much more.

Tremendous advances in technology are also disrupting established industries and economies. Remember the examples of the typewriter and the taxi industry? As a result, a lot of jobs we take for granted may simply be obsolete within the next ten years, or fewer. One respected futurist, Graeme Codrington, put it this way: "Private bankers and wealth managers will be replaced with algorithms.... Already we've stripped the financial industry of its most iconic personnel: the stock exchange floor traders. Now we've even taken most of the backroom traders away too, as stocks, currencies, and commodities are all traded by complex—and lightning fast—algorithms."[9]

"Lawyers, accountants, actuaries, and consulting engineers will be replaced with artificial intelligence....Any professional that is mainly involved in dealing with information is going to be replaced by algorithms and AI."[10]

Codrington is making an educated guess, of course, but he and others who look at these things may not be far off the mark. Another futurist, Joe Tankersley, sees a return or greater emphasis on local farming and agriculture as more and more people move to ever more remote places (society and work becoming more and more mobile, as they are), or perhaps even as they flock to more urban places.[11]

At the same time, however, technology is creating a host of new jobs and careers to replace the ones that are going away: remote health care specialists, neuro-implant technology and technicians, smart-home handymen, and 3-D printer design specialists.[12]

One thing the rapid rate of technological progress does guarantee is a high degree of uncertainty. No one can really know what jobs, products, or industries technology will render obsolete. That uncertainty should inform the decisions you make about your educational and career path.

While it is true the value of a college degree is much higher for an employment prospect than the value of a high school diploma, STEM degrees are clearly more valuable than others when it comes to looking for employment. When the Brookings Institution took a look at three measurements—mid-career earnings, occupational earnings (irrespective of whether they were in a high-paying career), and student loan repayment rates—they found it was not so much where you went to school that mattered but what you studied in school that mattered—and what mattered was STEM.[13]

One of the study's authors put it this way: "STEM is the biggest measurable factor on average across all the institutional factors.... The only surprising thing is that it works even if you don't go to an elite school. You don't necessarily have to go to Caltech or MIT and major in computer science there. Even if you go to community college, you'll see an earnings premium."[14]

In fact, here may be the most enticing headline anybody worried about paying back student loans could read: "Four Degrees with 0% Unemployment"![15] What are those degrees? Actuarial science (which is advanced math), astrophysics (which is advanced science), pharmacology (science), and geophysics (engineering and science).

Georgetown University's Center on Education and the Workforce crunched some data from the Census Bureau in 2015 to find the median salaries of college graduates over the course of their careers based on their majors. Here are a few of the highlights:

- Agriculture and natural resources: $82,000
- Architecture and engineering: $113,000
- Biology and life sciences: $83,000
- Computers, statistics, and mathematics: $107,000
- Physical sciences: $97,000
- Arts: $73,000
- Humanities and liberal arts: $78,000
- Psychology and social work: $69,000[16]

It's important to note that these are median salaries. And, of course, it would be impossible to determine a total value of a person engaged in, say, physical sciences versus education (where the median salary in 2015 was $59,000).

However, all else being equal, obtaining a solid foundation in STEM is the smart, forward-thinking move. Even if you plan on majoring in the humanities, it would be wise to minor in one of the STEM fields. You won't regret it, and as we've already seen, all industries are trending toward becoming tech industries. Journalism, teaching, business—name the field, and I could easily show how STEM would help you stand out in that field. But it's up to you to get the STEM education.

STATES INVESTING IN STEM CAREERS

Almost as important as understanding what fields of work provide the greatest opportunity is understanding where—literally—those jobs are. That, along with a host of other factors, should play a role in whether you move to Albuquerque or Austin after college (or *for* college).

Albuquerque, as it so happens, ranks seventy-seventh in number of ads for job openings with about 2,500 in a given quarter, according to the Brookings Institution. About 40 percent of those ads require STEM skills, placing it about forty-fifth in rankings for jobs requiring STEM skills. It also boasts average salaries of just over $57,000 in STEM fields.[17]

By contrast, Austin ranks twenty-seventh in total number of ads for job openings with almost 11,000 in a given quarter. About 48 percent of those ads require STEM skills, placing it ninth in jobs requiring STEM skills. It boasts average salaries of just over $62,000 in these STEM jobs—and you can find that almost three thousand of those job openings are in computer and mathematical sciences.[18]

Of course this is not the end of your set of considerations. As we saw earlier, you will want to look at such things as average rental prices or home prices, state taxes, and other factors such as proximity to family and friends. But you should know that a lot of states are taking new and active roles in attracting certain professions, skill sets, and career choices—and tailoring their educational institutions to foster them. States see the value in promoting their STEM industries because it's a great investment. Take Mississippi as just one example. As Chevron wrote in an advertisement in the *Atlantic Monthly* magazine:

> At Mississippi Gulf Coast Community College (MGCCC), the need for employees has pushed the administration to build new facilities to teach STEM skills. In the near future, the school will have 35,000 square feet of labs and other space dedicated solely to training welders, machinists and instrumentation control technicians, among other tech-driven occupations. Carmen Walters, the vice president of one of MGCCC's campuses, points to studies that show there will be some

46,000 available STEM jobs in the state by 2018. "We feel confident that STEM jobs are growing in Mississippi," she says. "Engineering and support jobs are well paid, and we want to train our students to get them."[19]

Whether you end up pursuing a STEM education in college or beyond is your choice. Plenty of students forgo a STEM education and find happiness and success in their preferred field and professions. But you shouldn't ignore the promise STEM education holds for most students, or deny the growing importance STEM fields will have in our new economy—one that is racing forward at a staggering pace. I cannot put it better than a STEM teacher who wrote the following in the *Washington Post*:

> STEM education is the opposite of specific, technical skills. Like a liberal arts education, it teaches thinking that promotes creativity, collaboration, skepticism and effective communication.... Science and math are more than facts that reflect our understanding of our natural world. They define a way of looking at the world in new ways that has served societies very well for 500 years. Likewise, technology and engineering are creative

processes that build ideas into realities that shape societies.[20]

I hope I've encouraged you to investigate STEM fields if you haven't done so already. But the opportunities in STEM careers aren't a secret. It's not a unique insight that engineering jobs pay more than other types of work. Knowing this puts you ahead of most of your peers, but there are still thousands who already know it. And they're going to pursue the same jobs as you are when you both graduate. Whether you pursue STEM or not, everyone entering the workforce in the new economy has to answer the same question: how will you distinguish yourself?

EIGHT

Don't Be a Commodity

Your parents' generation had a pretty clear set of guidelines for what careers would be most likely to bring financial stability and success. Law and medicine, in particular, were virtually guaranteed to be stable long-term jobs, and the post-graduation pathway was straightforward: go to graduate school, start a career, and move up the ladder from there.

While law and medicine remain good career choices, they aren't the sure things that they once were. The days when top graduates from elite law schools were lavishly courted and recruited by top national and international law firms are mostly a thing of the past. Many of those firms have closed and many of the largest firms have cut employees and hiring programs just as they retire some of their most experienced and well-known practitioners in order to save money. Eighty-five percent of law school graduates carry at least $100,000 in debt, but in 2014 more than 180 of the top 200 law schools in the United States were unable to find jobs for more than 80 percent of their graduates, and median salaries are down 17 percent for the lucky few who do manage to find work in the industry.[1]

One former law student actually resorted to suing her law school for "fraud." The plaintiff had graduated in the top tier of her class and passed the state bar, but ten years later she had been unable to find a job. The case made head-lines around the country because this was the first of its kind—and no doubt many felt sympathy for the former student who had $170,000 in student loans. Regardless, she lost.[2]

It's not just Big Law that's taking a hit. Small firms and solo practitioners are struggling even more. In 1988, solo practitioners earned an inflation-adjusted $70,747, but by 2012 that number had fallen to $49,130, a 30 percent decrease in real income. That number is the average income for lawyers filing as solo practitioners, not a starting salary.[3] That is still a good salary, but hardly exceptional for some-one who has spent seven years (and borrowed tens of thou-sands of dollars in student loans) earning a law degree.

Meanwhile, changes in technology and policy have transformed the way medicine is practiced and delivered.

Doctors find themselves struggling to navigate a regulatory landscape that hinders their freedom of action. Medical practices must comply with rules that force doctors to treat patients in a certain, preapproved way. I'm not saying this is right or wrong. Health care is a notoriously complicated field and the infusion of digital technologies, once believed to be the cure for the confusion, have done little to make it any easier. One result of the mess is that more medical students choose highly specialized fields over the less lucrative path of primary care,[4] and fewer students seek medicine as a career on the whole. In fact, according to the American Association of Medical Colleges, our health care system could be facing a shortage of nearly 100,000 doctors by 2025.[5]

I do not want to discourage you from studying law or medicine and entering those fields. I simply want to point out that they are not what they once were. Going into those fields to make a living is a harder proposition than it used to be. If you love the idea of practicing law, go there. If you love the idea of practicing medicine, pursue that. But understand that in a new economic and cultural landscape, those fields are simply not the big money-makers or guaranteed areas of employment they once were.

But even if you pursue those fields, one thing you should know is that your formal education likely won't be enough to succeed. What I mean is that the years you spend at law or medical school will teach you how to be a lawyer or doctor. What they won't teach you is how to be a lawyer or doctor in the new economy. That's up to you.

And the same holds true for every other imaginable profession. Even if you think your dream job has a specific course, one where you'll learn everything you need to know to perform it, you're wrong. As you read earlier, although Juliana was usually the smartest person in the room, she still had to learn how to lead a team. You don't learn leadership in algebra. You don't learn self-management in law or medical school. Likewise, don't think that you'll necessarily learn what you need to know "on the job." As we saw in the previous chapter, employers need college graduates to hit the ground running.

The question is how.

COMMODITY VS. SPECIALTY PRODUCT

You've probably heard the word "commodity"—an economic term for a product or good, usually a raw material or agricultural item that can be bought or sold. One of the defining characteristics of a commodity is that it doesn't have quality differentiation in the market. For example, wheat is a commodity. The market sets the price, and Acme Agriculture's bushel of wheat will sell to the market for the same price as ABC Agriculture's wheat. In other words, wheat is wheat. That's a commodity.

Don't be a commodity.

What I mean is that simply having a college degree doesn't set you apart. It may differentiate you from a high school graduate, but college graduates and high school graduates aren't pursuing the same jobs. What you need to be able to ⬚⬚⬚⬚⬚⬚⬚⬚ ⬚⬚⬚⬚f from the roughly two million ⬚⬚⬚⬚⬚⬚⬚⬚⬚⬚⬚⬚⬚ege every year, and millio⬚⬚⬚⬚⬚⬚⬚⬚⬚⬚⬚⬚⬚e workforce.

⬚⬚⬚⬚⬚⬚⬚⬚⬚⬚⬚⬚⬚⬚⬚The workforce has changed. More A⬚⬚⬚⬚⬚⬚⬚a college degree than ever before, not just because college is more accessible, but also because they simply need a degree. Many agricultural and manufacturing workers have been replaced with machines. The people who used to do these jobs must now compete for other jobs—and these jobs require more training and skills. As a result, the workforce in general is smarter than it used to be; even the lowest-wage jobs require skills more highly specialized than the lowest-wage jobs did fifty years ago. And with college open to so many, even manufacturing workers can get a degree from a two-year institution or trade school and get a far better job than their parents had.

Where I'm going with this discussion is that a college degree is not the differentiator it once was; it's the *bare minimum*. As we saw in the last chapter, employers are lamenting that college graduates don't possess the skills that are needed in today's advanced workplace. When they leave college, graduates are like commodities—very little differences between them. And just like with any commodity, employers will buy (that is, hire) the cheapest one.

Instead of being a commodity, one of tens of millions of potential employees with a college degree, you want to be a specialty product—a product uniquely different from its competitors. And it's this unique difference that makes the specialty product *more valuable* than its competitors.

For instance, take a cell phone. There didn't used to be many differences between telephones. Sure, businesses needed multiple lines and a "hold" feature, but for the average consumer, a phone was a phone. Then cell phones hit and suddenly a phone wasn't just a phone anymore. One could take pictures, while another allowed you to access the Internet. One was smaller and slimmer than the other.

Now we're at the point where the telephone feature of a cell phone is the *bare minimum*; you better be offering something more than that if you want to sell your phones. That's because cell phones have become specialty products—each one is different than its competitors. That's the point. Those differences are trying to entice the consumer to buy it. Maybe you value a bigger screen over faster service, so you buy Acme's phone instead of ABC's.

And price plays a role as well. If you want the best phone, you'll pay the most money. If all you need is a mobile phone, then you can get one very cheaply. But to say that the cheapest phone is the same as the best phone simply because they're *both phones* is absurd.

There was a time when a college degree was enough of a competitive advantage. Those days are gone. If all you have is a college degree, then you're a commodity—plain and simple. You need to leave college as a specialty product. You need to be offering future employers something more than the *bare minimum*.

WHAT GOOGLE LOOKS FOR

As I mentioned earlier, Google is a company that epitomizes the new economy, as a tech company that also has blurred the lines with other industries. I had the privilege of speaking with a member of the Google team, Adam Swidler. Adam is a product marketing manager at Google who agreed to talk with me about what Google looks for when it's hiring—and Google is always hiring. What he said deserves to be quoted in full:

> Fundamentally, we are looking for people who are very strong in a set of cognitive, analytic abilities as well as a set of creative, energetic, passion areas. Let me start first with the general cognitive ability stuff. We call our ideal candidates "smart creatives," people that have grown up along with

technology. They know that all the information's available at their fingertips and that the recipe for success within Google is to create small teams of people that are passionate about a particular thing that lines up with management strategy, and enable them to go and tackle that particular problem.

There are thousands of these little teams at Google working on something, whether it's a new feature for a particular product or whether it's a new product that we're rolling out. We're looking for people that can apply a rich set of analytic skills, especially to large quantities of data, and access that set of information to ask interesting questions about their task or problem.

We're not necessarily looking for deep domain expertise in a particular area. We're really looking for people who show an aptitude to pick up a new area quickly, to think creatively about different approaches, especially different ways that technology could solve that particular problem. Then we want them to have a mindset around testing and prototyping, and getting things into the hands of the users as quickly as possible to get feedback from the users.

We're looking for people who can bring those types of tools together. We're going to want them to bring it to us in an environment that's highly collaborative. We want people who want to share their idea with the team as soon as they get it.

We give candidates wonderful general cognitive tests. For instance: You're an elevator design officer with a specific constraint in the building. Now tell me how you go about designing this elevator system. There's no right answer. Rather, what we want to see is a creative intuition. We love to see how their minds work, how they tackle the problem of this elevator design with one quirky constraint.

Even though we stress collaboration, we're also looking for candidates who tackle problems without being asked to. We love our employees to say, "I didn't know what to do, so I set up experiment A, experiment B, experiment C, and here's how I measured the results; and here's why I think this is the best course of action." During interviews, we throw out these crazy problems and just sit back and let them puzzle through it.

We're always looking for people who can also take a step back to see the bigger picture, to see opportunities. At Google in particular, there's very little role relegation. You don't have to stay in your role. We want our employees to go outside their role and do what they think needs to be done, or at least go convince management that they should do what needs to be done.

I think Adam's answer perfectly captures the type of "professional skills" today's graduate needs to succeed, not just at Google, but anywhere. You might be saying to yourself: "Well, that's Google! I can't work there." Yes, Google is highly selective. But the reason I've stressed it so prominently is because it has become so much the archetype of the twenty-first century company. In other words, if you possess the skills Google values, then you'll thrive in nearly any environment.

THE NEW SKILLS OF THE NEW ECONOMY

I wanted you to read Adam's words on their own before I supplied my own interpretation. You might read it very differently than I read it, and that's okay. But now let's compare notes. Here are the skills I heard when I listened to Adam talk:

Intra-**preneurial Leadership**: With the stunning careers of Mark Zuckerberg, Bill Gates, and Steve Jobs, the entrepreneur has come to define the new economy. But not everyone has the desire or the ability to start her own business—and that's a good thing. So what defines an entrepreneur other than starting her own business? Leadership. The ability to tackle a specific problem and organize a team to find a solution. That's what I heard Adam say when he spoke about "smart creatives." The challenges facing any one company are more than any single person can solve. Which is why it's the person who can successfully lead a team from problem identification to solution who would be extremely valuable at any company.

Self-Management: The other big point I kept hearing Adam make was this idea that Google expects its employees to act independently. The reason Google has very little "role relegation" is that they don't want people saying, "That isn't my job." They want their people to feel confident going after a problem, regardless if the problem falls into their purview. This attitude follows a trend in the new economy that has led companies toward a less hierarchical, flatter organizational structure. The focus has been taken off middle managers to manage their team, and on to team members to think and act on their own. We shouldn't underestimate the pressure this puts on the employee, nor should we underestimate the power today's employees have, at least compared to the average employee twenty or thirty years ago. Simply put, today's employees have more computing power at their fingertips than NASA did during the entire first moon landing. But to use this power requires an ability to know how to manage one's self. Software and the latest devices only go so far in their ability to foster productivity; the rest, and it's the largest chunk, is up to the worker. The worker who can't self-manage will soon find himself out of a job.

Data Analytics: The final piece I heard from Adam is the rising importance of being able to read and understand hard data. Clearly, this isn't as exciting as the first two—and certainly requires more formal education. As discussed in the previous chapter, digital data are the fuel powering the new economy. In the business world, the power and promise of digital data go under the term "Big Data." It's an amorphous phrase that does little to underscore just how important data analysis is and will be in the new economy. One report on the "Digital Universe" puts the importance of Big Data on new business trends well:

> [E]nterprises are finding new sources of data, new ways to analyze data, new ways to apply the analysis to the business, and new revenues for themselves as a result. They are using new approaches, moving from descriptive to predictive and prescriptive analytics and doing data analysis in real-time. They are also increasingly adopting self-service business intelligence and analytics, giving executives and frontline workers easy-to-use software tools for data discovery and timely decision-making. [6]

In today's economy, to succeed is to have a certain degree of "data literacy." The next phase of innovative gadgets, products, and platforms will be founded on creative interpretation of new (and old) data sets. Today's college graduates must exhibit a familiarity with analyzing data sets and discovering opportunities.

We could certainly grow this list, but we'll start there. I want you to keep this list in mind as you enter college and progress through your courses. You may not be able to take a course on "Intra-prenuerial Leadership," but if you're a math major, for example, it would probably help to take a business course or two, which should stress team building and collaboration. To acquire these skills you'll have to get creative in your own education, but that's the point. It's *your education*. Take control of it.

College is your time to gain the best education you can. You can't be a passive participant. You can't simply cross off the requirements for your major and degree and think that you're now ready to enter the workforce. Remember, all you've done is the *bare minimum*. You're still a commodity. Instead, you must progress through your college years with a firm goal in mind: to become a specialty product. We're going to get into how to do that in the next section. For now, it's enough for you to understand that you must do it.

NINE

Why College?

What are three things that Bill Gates, Mark Zuckerberg, and the late Steve Jobs had in common? First, each one played a major role in creating the new economy you will soon enter. Second, they all made their fortunes before they hit thirty. Third, they all dropped out of college. Some people have connected these commonalities and think they see a pattern. Some people seem to think Jobs, Gates, and Zuckerberg became wildly successful *because* they dropped out of college. Therefore, one road to riches and stratospheric success is to drop out of college.

The problem with this analysis is that it uses an extremely small sample size. The reason we know about famous college dropouts is because there simply aren't that many of them, at least compared to *non-famous* college dropouts. In fact, it's not even close. We'll get to why in a moment.

On the other hand, there is more than enough evidence to show that a college degree vastly improves one's earning potential over one's lifetime.

Here's a question for you: who is Peter Thiel? If you use PayPal, then you might know him as one of the service's founders. He also invested early in Facebook, which was a good move. These days, Thiel works more on the funding side of start-ups and wears many hats: hedge-fund manager, venture capitalist, and author. Like the others, Thiel too found success at a very young age. Unlike the other three, however, Thiel did graduate from college—from Stanford, in fact, with a BA in philosophy.

It's a bit ironic, then, that Thiel created a program that encourages students to drop out of college. The Thiel Fellowship, which he launched in 2010, awards thirty college students under the age of twenty-two with $100,000 to drop out of school and pursue their entrepreneurial dreams. In addition to the money, paid out over two years, the fellowship also provides the winners with other resources and guidance.

In 2015, the fellowship reported that a record 2,800 students had applied for the award, and little wonder. The eighty former Thiel Fellows collectively have raised more than $142 million in venture capital and generated $41 million in revenue.[1] The Thiel Fellowship, if one is talented enough to win it, seems to be a fast track to riches and success.

Explaining the idea behind the fellowship, Thiel once said that for too many students, college is a waste of time. He continued:

> I feel I was personally very guilty of this; you don't know what to do with your life, so you get a college degree; you don't know what you're going to do with your college degree, so you get a graduate degree. In my case it was law school, which is the classic thing one does when one has no idea what else to do. I don't have any big regrets, *but if I had to do it over I would try to think more about the future than I did at the time.* [Emphasis added][2]

After reading the first eight chapters of this book, it may surprise you to know that I completely agree with Thiel's statement. Too many young people "don't know what to do with [their] life, so [they] get a college degree." They do what they think they're supposed to, with no further thought as to why they're doing it.

That's a problem because, as you now know, college is an expensive way to discover yourself. And for the type of person who stands a chance of winning a Thiel Fellowship, perhaps college is a waste of time. But here's something I want you to understand: college *will* be a waste of time for anyone who doesn't "think more about the future," as Thiel said he wishes he had done.

As should be clear to you by now, this book is intended to make you think a little bit deeper about your adult life. It's meant to make you question the shallow advice you've received about "following your dreams." It's meant to open your eyes to the reality of life that awaits you when you enter the adult world. As we saw earlier, it's not very pretty—but it's only a surprise for those who face the future with their eyes closed.

And, finally, this book is meant to help you approach college in the right way—with the right expectations, the right goals, and, hopefully, the right outcomes. So we'll also look a bit deeper at what awaits you at college, starting with whether you should go to college at all. We'll walk through the steps of picking the right college for you. We'll also focus on how you should best spend your time at college, both in and out of the classroom. Our goal at the end of this section is to make sure you have a plan on how to make the most out of your college years so that when you do enter that intimidating world economy, you'll be ready.

STAY HUNGRY. STAY FOOLISH. STAY IN COLLEGE.

The Thiel Fellowship is aimed at a certain type of student—and this type of student is exceedingly rare. The simple fact is most people aren't Steve Jobs, Bill Gates, Mark Zuckerberg, or Peter Thiel. This isn't a comment on their intelligence; there are *a lot* of very smart people who aren't successful millionaires (or billionaires). Thiel is trying to make it easier for the really smart people to become really successful people too. When you hear advice from this type of person, you need to understand that his or her experience is wildly different from what yours is likely to be.

As the creator and driving force behind the meteoric rise of Apple, Steve Jobs is credited with what may be the most famous commencement speech in recent memory. At Stanford University in 2005, Jobs explained why he dropped out of college and ended with this advice: "And most important, have the courage to follow your heart and intuition. They somehow already know what you truly want to become. Everything else is secondary." He concluded by charging the graduates to "Stay hungry. Stay foolish."[3]

You should know by now that I don't entirely agree with Jobs here. No one in the audience that day could have taken Jobs's advice to mean they should drop out of college—they were just graduating, after all. But millions more young people have likely heard about or read Jobs's advice to "stay hungry, stay foolish" and concluded that, since the founder of Apple did it, they too could drop out of college and follow their dreams. Maybe others have decided to avoid college all together.

Especially when you add up college's high cost, the idea that one doesn't "need" it is probably more popular than ever before. Recent studies give some evidence that this is happening. As *The New York Times* reported in 2013:

> More than 70 percent of Americans matriculate at a four-year college—the seventh-highest rate among 23 developed nations for which the O.E.C.D. compiles such statistics. But less than two-thirds end up graduating. Including community colleges, the graduation rate drops to 53 percent. Only Hungary does worse.[4]

To be blunt: dropping out of college is a terrible idea. Study after study confirms this. A 2014 Pew Research study is unequivocal in its conclusions: "On virtually every measure of economic well-being and career attainment—from personal earnings to job satisfaction to the share employed full time—young college graduates are outperforming their peers with less education."[5]

A similar study from the Federal Reserve Bank of San Francisco is just as clear about the long-term benefits of a college degree. The study found that the so-called college earnings premium—how much more one makes because of a college degree—averages about $20,000. This has remained mostly unchanged for decades. But this also is misleading, as the study readily admits:

It's also important to remember that investing in college, like investing in a house or a business, is a long-term prospect...new college graduates start out earning just a little more ($5,000 to $6,000) than high school graduates. Over time, this earnings gap grows markedly, so that after 15 years it's over $25,000 per year. This means that comparing the current salaries of recent college graduates with those of people who started working right after high school won't tell you that much about the future.[6]

In fact, over the course of a lifetime, a college degree is worth $365,000 for the average American man and $185,000 for the average American woman. That's even when you subtract all the direct and indirect costs, like tuition.

And while we've seen how the new economy has put a lot of pressure on recent college graduates, the pay gap between those with a degree and those without continues to grow. According to an analysis of Labor Department statistics by the Economic Policy Institute, U.S. workers with a four-year degree made 98 percent more on average than those without a degree in 2013. That's nine points higher than in 2010, thirteen points higher than in 2005, and thirty-four points higher than in the early 1980s.[7]

We don't need to belabor the point; there is no debate about the merits of a college education. Stay hungry, but get your degree. Stay foolish, but get your degree. Stay in college, so that you can earn your degree.

THE FOUR-YEAR ALTERNATIVES

There is also a growing debate about *what type* of college one should attend. Back when I was beginning college, there were two main alternatives to the four-year institution: trade schools and community colleges. Of course these still exist today, but they've been joined by a third alternative: online universities. In fact, many community colleges, which offer two-year associate degrees, have put their courses online.

Not so long ago, online universities were perceived in the same way as the trade school or community college—something far inferior to the four-year institution. This has changed. Indeed, one of the greatest things to happen to higher education in the last twenty years has been the growing popularity and quality of the alternatives to four-year institutions. Competition is good for any market—but it's been particularly good for higher education.

Why? Two reasons. First, higher education, especially accredited institutions that provide four-year degrees, produce an indispensable product. As we just saw, there is no comparison between the earning power of a college gradu-ate and that of a high school graduate. Far more than just a mark of accomplished learning, the four-year degree will open doors. An applicant with a degree instantly gains access to jobs with salaries that are mostly unavailable to high school graduates.

But as we saw earlier, many employers have begun to question whether the four-year degree signifies someone who is ready for the challenges of the new economy. They wouldn't be thinking that if more universities had updated their curricula to reflect the economy's changing demands. Four-year alternatives have stepped into the gap to offer students a more focused and specialized education. And this isn't just for students who wish to learn a particular trade or become nurses or teachers. After all, what is the motivation behind the Thiel Fellowship other than the growing notion that colleges and universities in general are failing to prepare their students for the twenty-first-century economy?

The hope is that the existence of these alternatives will force more universities and colleges to update their curricula and course offerings to better reflect the unique challenges of the new economy. We'll see some examples of this in the next chapter, but in practice this would involve a recogni-tion that subjects cannot be entirely separate entities any-more. So, for instance, writing courses wouldn't be confined to the English Department, but would also be offered in the Math Department, tailored for those who enter a career in mathematics. As in the new economy, so in education: the convergence of industries requires a convergence of academic subjects.

The second reason the rise of online colleges has been a good thing is that colleges and universities are aware they provide an indispensable product that no one else does. And when one produces an indispensable product, one can charge *a lot* for it. This isn't the only reason tuition rates have been rising dramatically in recent decades, but it's certainly a big factor. With easily available student loans, there has been very little economic pressure against rising prices. This near-monopoly presents students, particularly poorer ones, with a bad deal: to earn this indispensable product, you must take out loans and go into debt. Many students have decided that it's not worth it.

That said, the traditional four-year institution remains the superior choice for most students. While I believe the U.S. higher education system is the best in the world, I appreciate how alternative models have provided competition and are driving change in the university system. Many traditional universities now offer extensive online courses and degrees, and we are fast approaching a time when an entirely online degree is perceived as indistinguishable from its campus-based counterparts.

This is why I would advise you to view your options as generations in the past have viewed them. That is to say, if your career goals only require a two-year associate's degree or one you can acquire online, then don't waste money on a four-year institution. Just be sure that the path you choose and the skills you develop will prepare you to navigate the new economy for decades to come.

HOW TO CHOOSE YOUR SCHOOL

The next great question you need to answer is what school is best for you. If you're already going through this process, then you're aware about the multitude of resources to help you decide. I'm not going to get into the merits of one school over another. I'm not going to say that you should go to a state school over a private liberal arts school. Rather, I'm going to dispel some myths that have grown up around where you go to school.

MYTH #1: COLLEGE RANKINGS MATTER

Here's the truth about college rankings that should alleviate some of the pressure you might feel in choosing the right school: unless you have the opportunity to attend a Top Twenty-Five college or university, don't worry about rankings.

U.S. News and World Report's annual college ranking, considered the *sine qua non* of rankings, almost always lists the same schools in the Top Twenty-Five every year. Within this elite tier, you'll find the Ivy League schools, as well as a handful of other institutions that compete with one another for every spot. It's a big deal for these schools to move up in the rankings, because it means that they'll get more applications from the world's best students. It's also a big deal when a school breaks into the Top Twenty-Five or leaves it.

Here's what you need to know. Yes, if you have the opportunity to go to an Ivy League school or one of the others that are usually in the Top Twenty-Five, then go. Get your loans, if you need them, and go. The reason I say this is because having a degree from one of these Top Twenty-Five schools will help with future employers—in some cases for the rest of your life. A Harvard graduate is a Harvard graduate forever and most businesses would love to have a Harvard graduate. The same is true for MIT, Yale, Stanford, and Princeton. If a four-year degree opens doors, a degree from one of these schools opens gates to some of the most exclusive circles in the world. The quality of education at any of these schools is the best the world has to offer, no matter what your chosen major or profession.

The flip side is that these are also the most selective schools in the world and it is exceedingly difficult to be accepted, if you even apply. These schools reject hundreds of valedictorians every year, so it's no shame to be denied admission. But that leaves all the other students with a problem: should they go to the best-ranked school (below the Top Twenty-Five) that they can get into?

Answer: no.

The simple truth is that few employers care about where you went to school, unless you went to a Top Twenty-Five. And they care less and less the older you get. By the time you're thirty, no employer is going to hire you because you went to the thirty-eighth ranked school. Or the seventy-eighth ranked school. Or the two-hundred-and-thirty-eighth ranked school. By then, your work experience and accomplishments will speak for themselves.

Yes, but what about right out of college? Even right out of college, when all you have on your resume (or LinkedIn profile) is where you went to school, employers won't give where you went to school more weight than your major and work history. Are there exceptions? Sure, of course, but they aren't worth stressing about while you agonize over what school to attend.

Rather, your choice of school should be decided on three factors:

1. **Cost:** Don't spend an extra $100,000 for the private school simply because it's ranked

fortieth when you can just as easily attend a state school. Other things being equal, the benefits will not outweigh the costs to you after graduation. Likewise, if you're offered financial aid to attend one school, then you should consider it seriously.

2. **Major:** Far more important than a school's ranking is its strength and reputation in certain subjects. If you want to pursue engineering, then you should focus your search on schools with strong engineering programs, and forget its overall ranking. This should seem obvious, except that there are incredibly strong schools out there that don't get a lot of media attention.

3. **Alumni support:** This is one area that most students won't ever consider until they've graduated, but that's a mistake. The built-in network one gains by being a graduate of a college or university will do just as much to open doors as the degree. Moreover, when I say "alumni support," I include the relationships the institution has with certain companies and industries—usually made possible because of alumni. It is these relationships that can help a student receive invaluable work experience while still in college. Likewise, upon graduation, this alumni network will prove indispensable.

MYTH #2: WHERE YOU GO WILL AFFECT THE REST OF YOUR LIFE

It's hard to avoid the feeling when you're applying to college that the decision you eventually make will be life-altering. It will be, and as perhaps your first life-altering decision, you are right to be worried about it. But too many high school students despair if they don't get into their first choice, as if somehow their lives are permanently changed for the worse.

Failing to get into your first choice of school is a good life lesson. You learn that you can't have everything you want in life, and this will eventually teach you that that's okay. Let me put it this way: almost no one in the adult world really thinks that their lives are worse because of where they *didn't go to school.* As I said above, by age thirty your life experiences and work history will matter far more than your alma mater.

More to the point, *what you do* at college matters more than where you go. If you use the three factors I mentioned above, then you should have a variety of options, none any better or worse than the other. Of course you can have your favorite, but if all you have is your favorite, then you're not doing it right. Every school on your list will have its strengths and weaknesses: one will be more expensive, one will have the better electrical engineering program, and one will have great relationships with quality companies. Sit down with your parents or guidance counselor to decide which one makes the most sense for you. Then make your decision and go for it.

Let's talk about graduate school, too, for a moment. If you already know that you want or need an advanced degree, then you should factor that into your undergraduate application process. What I mean is that employers, to the extent they care at all, will only care about your most recent school. If you go to graduate school, then that's the school that most employers will notice. This is important because you'll likely be saddled with a lot of student loan debt after your studies, so it would be wiser to save some money on your undergraduate degree and go to a state school, in the hopes of attending a more prestigious graduate program later.

The point is that you shouldn't get discouraged. The most important thing about college isn't where you went, but *what you learned*.

Now, on to the learning part.

TEN

Your Four Years

ere's a sobering statistic: if you attend a public university, the odds of graduating in four years with a
bachelor's degree are against you. A 2014 report
found that only 19 percent of full time students at public
universities earn their degree in four years. The report also
found that only fifty of more than 580 public four-year
universities graduate a majority of their full-time students
on time.[1]

We've already seen that paying off your student loans is
perhaps your biggest concern after graduation. Every semester you spend in college you will likely add thousands of
dollars to your student loan debt, which is why you want to
spend as little time in college as you possibly can. We might

laugh at those students who are on the "five- or six-year plan," but it won't be funny the moment those students gets their first student loan bills.

I have a theory that we could radically improve the four-year graduation rate across the country if students had to pay per class. I'm not talking about a course; rather, I'm talking about all the classes you're required to attend in a given course. Under this system, you would have to pay for every class you take, whether you attend class or not. This "pay-as-you-go" system would vary depending on institution, but you'd be looking at a per-class check somewhere between fifty to one hundred dollars.

This new payment system would likely have two effects. First, many students would simply drop out of college. They would conclude (wrongly) that what they pay for each course isn't worth it. The other, better effect would be that those students who remain would want to get the most out of each class they attend. They would look at their college experience as the accumulation of education, not as the price to pay for four years of fun. Each class would have an immediate value attached to it, which would force students to look at courses as something they're "buying"—not something they have to pass to get a degree.

Under this system, students would approach their studies in a far more economical way than they do currently. A student who knows the value of each class would choose the classes that are of the most value to him. What constitutes "value" to an individual student varies, of course. What's valuable to an English major won't be as valuable to an engineering major.

But there's more to planning your classes than just simply the matter of majors. Universities and colleges do a good job of guiding a student along a four-year path toward a degree in their major. As you'll find, however, that's not the entirety of the college experience. You will have the time and freedom to choose courses outside your major (and that's where the "pay-as-you-go" system would prove most effective).

Of course we don't have a "pay-as-you-go" higher education system. In reality, it would be cumbersome and unrealistic. But I want you to look at your college life as if we did have this system. If you fully understand and appreciate the cost of each class, you will likely graduate in four years. You will also graduate with the necessary educational foundation to begin a successful career.

FOUR YEARS, 120 CREDITS

So the question is: how do we begin calculating the cost per class? It's not nearly as hard as it might sound. Most four-year institutions require 120 credits to graduate with a bachelor's degree. You usually get one credit for each hour you spend in class per week. For example, if you take four three-hour classes per week, then you're taking twelve credits that semester. Each semester is about sixteen weeks, which means you take about 192 classes per semester, give or take.

Recall that I said that the average tuition of a four-year public university was $17,474. That means that each semester costs $8,737. Now it's a simple matter of dividing that number by the number of classes in a semester. So in this example, we have:

$8,737/192 (classes) = $45.51

In this analysis, our hypothetical student pays $45.51 for every class he takes. Yours will differ, of course. For example, the average tuition of a four-year private university is $35,074, each semester costing $17,537. Therefore:

$17,537/192 (classes) = $91.34

When you calculate your number, I want you to memorize it. This is the money you are throwing away every time you choose to sleep in and skip class, goof off in class, or watch a movie on your smartphone. It's simple math. But I would encourage you to do more than simply acknowledge the cost every time you attend (or don't attend) class. I would advise that you keep a tally in a simple spreadsheet and enter the cost every time you attend class. That way you can see the cost of your college education start to add up. That number will start to get very big, very quickly—a potent reminder of what you're investing in your education.

Now let's dig a little deeper into those 120 credits. Most programs require you to take a fairly rigid set of forty to sixty credits for a given major. That represents between a third and a half of your overall credits. You should set that aside. While you'll have a measure of choice in how to spend those credits, you're working within the rules of your department and there won't be much flexibility. Rather, the bigger concern is what you're going to do with the rest of your credits.

A lot of colleges and universities, especially those with a liberal arts focus, will require that you satisfy certain requisites, such as a history or language requirement. Like the requirements for your major, this is unavoidable. We'll discuss in a moment the value of a liberal arts education, but for now let's just assume that you have about a third or so credits left. These are your so-called "elective" credits.

How you choose to spend these credits, which will cost you several thousand dollars, is what will set you apart from your peers. You see, most students attend college just to do what they need to do to graduate. They satisfy their major requirements, but give little to no thought to the rest of their college course work. They take elective courses that seem interesting, but with no real reason or forethought. This is a waste of money and a missed opportunity.

This is why I urge you to put a price tag on each class you attend. If you do that, then you won't waste a class on something that won't return any possible value to you. For example, you might be a biology major who has a curiosity about nineteenth-century English literature. Would you spend several thousand dollars on a course that satisfies a mere curiosity, especially when you could satisfy that curiosity with a whole host of inexpensive books and free online resources?

On the other hand, let's look at the same problem from an English major's perspective. You should already know that your earning potential after graduation is about half of your engineering peers, so your objective should be to distinguish yourself from your other English majors by acquiring as many marketable skills as possible. Would taking a course on microbiology do that? Probably not. As an English major, you're not looking for a job in biology after graduation. (At least you shouldn't be.) You're probably going to find yourself looking at the media industry. And you know where most people consume their media: on the Internet and digital devices. This fact alone should give you some guidance on what sort of elective courses to take; computer science, coding, or media marketing. Complement your major with useful knowledge; satisfy your intellectual curiosity in other ways.

You will never get those credits back. The "cost-per-class" framework isn't just dollars and cents—it's a matter of spending the most precious resource in the world: time. You can spend the rest of your life indulging in your curiosity about Charles Dickens or micro-organisms. But you won't have the rest of your life to prepare for your post-college career. You have four years. Four years to prepare yourself for the employment challenges ahead. Above all, do whatever you can to distinguish yourself from your peers, particularly your fellow biology or English majors.

THE GREAT COURSE CONVERGENCE

As I've stated continually throughout this book, my intention isn't to push you toward STEM. I want you to make the best informed decision possible about college and career and that means I have told you the simple truth about STEM education and jobs. I'm also not going to tell you which major is best for you. Earlier we discussed average salaries of particular majors, but that's about all I'm going to say on that topic. You know your goals and dreams. I hope that you're thinking about those goals and dreams in a smarter way than you had previously, with an eye on practical matters like debt and expenses. Maybe you've decided to look into other fields because of what you've read; or maybe you're just as committed to a specific career path, only a bit wiser and with more realistic expectations.

Wherever you find yourself, there are certain skills and assets you should still acquire, no matter your major or career dreams. As we discussed in chapter eight, the "new skills of the new economy" are *intra*-preneurial leadership, self-management, and data analytics, but we didn't really discuss how to acquire these skills. They can only truly be learned and mastered through work experience, but that doesn't mean you can't get a head start as a student.

For starters, you can begin to learn these skills by using your extra credits, those "electives" mentioned above, wisely. I want to stress that these skills are the same whether you're a math or English major, whether you want to design jet engines or build the next Facebook. How can this be? Well, as we mentioned before, one feature of the new economy is the convergence of industries. For example, Ford is now also a tech company and Google is now also a car company. That's an oversimplification, but you get the idea. The same technologies are spreading through and changing nearly every industry on the planet, and one consequence of this is that workers use the same skills no matter where they work. A computer science graduate doesn't have to work for Apple or Dell; he can work for basically any company that uses computer technologies—in other words, all of them.

Education should reflect this great convergence—only it doesn't. Nearly every four-year university or college maintains separate departments (or even separate schools) for its main subjects: math, English, biology, computer science, engineering, etc. But this compartmentalization of subjects doesn't reflect the new economy. In today's biology labs, students should have a working knowledge of computer science. A math major who goes to work for a company as a data analyst should be able to articulate his findings in a clear, uncomplicated way to his non-mathematical bosses, which means he should know how to write. A computer science major with the next great idea for an app should know the basics of going about starting a business, even if that isn't part of the course requirements for her major.

Is it starting to make sense? No matter your major or career goals, there are some skills relevant to the new economy that will not only serve you well after graduation; they'll distinguish you from your peers. An English major who understands coding, a math major who can write, a computer science student who knows about business finances—these are the cross-functional skills sets employers look for, and the very things university departments don't do a great job facilitating. In other words, you won't be required to learn to write a decent proposal as a math major. You won't be graded on your understanding of accounting as a computer science major. None of your English professors will teach you how to design a website that takes advantage of the latest in digital media.

It's up to you to learn these things. And I'm going to make it a bit easier for you. Here are three skills you should acquire in college, no matter your major or career focus.

1. **Communication:** If you can write well, you have a place in most any office in the country.

The ability to write is fast becoming a lost art, although, ironically, we write more than ever these days. From our smartphones to our social media profiles to daily emails, we're constantly writing. And yet most of us do a terrible job of it. Worse, we're allowed to graduate college without proving we can write competently. You must take it upon yourself to learn how to write. I'm not talking about creative writing or studying Shakespeare. I'm talking about taking English composition and other similar courses that will teach you how to be a more effective communicator. It is no overstatement to say that the one skill that will set you above your peers is your ability to write well. For this reason alone, you must learn to write.

2. **Business Administration:** Management, marketing, finance. These essentials of business administration will serve you well no matter what profession you pursue, because they will begin your education in two of the "new skills of the new economy" we discussed earlier: *intra*-preneurial leadership and self-management. Employers need people who know the basics of business. They need to know that you can handle a spreadsheet, manage a small team, and solve a problem without being told how to do it.

What's more, many undergraduate business courses will put you into small teams to accomplish a certain task. This is invaluable experience, which will prepare you for the type of working environments you will find outside of school. The goal with this skill isn't to master business administration; rather, it's to help you familiarize yourself with what happens inside a business and why. The applicant who already knows this and can talk about it intelligently will stand out.

3. **Computer Literacy:** I use the word "literacy" here as a catch-all, because we're actually talking about a lot of technical skills: coding, analytics, mathematics, computational and creative thinking. In general, everyone going into the new economy for the first time should know something about how computers work and function. I'm not saying that you have to be a master coder or computer programmer. Instead, you should be able to understand basic computer procedures and practices. You should know how our digital devices work and why we use them for specific tasks. Your basic computer science course will cover a lot of this, but I would encourage you to delve deeper in some specific aspect that relates well to your

career aspirations. If you don't have any idea what that would be, then you should ask your professor or someone who already works in your field. How are digital technologies changing the career you want to enter? If you can answer that question, then you should have a good idea of what area of computer science to focus on.

By no means do these three skills exhaust the opportunities to complement your major. But they give you a place to start. They should make you think a bit more carefully about how you want to spend your "elective" time during your four years. We haven't discussed double majors or minors, but clearly these are ways you can highlight your second-level knowledge. Even then, you will have to prove your proficiency in these skills. There are few moments in life as satisfying as when your boss wants to know if "anyone can do this" and you raise your hand to say, "Yes, I can do that."

THE LIBERAL ARTS QUESTION

In 1988 a book exploded on the higher education scene called *The Closing of the American Mind*, written by a university professor named Allan Bloom. The gist of the book, still in print, was Bloom's contention that "higher education has failed democracy and impoverished the souls of today's students." In particular, Bloom lashed out at the moral relativism that had taken over the humanities departments of America's leading universities. These "new age" professors brought with them modern works to replace the classics that comprised the Western canon. A professor of philosophy, Bloom championed the idea of the "liberally educated person." As he wrote:

> A liberal education means precisely helping students to pose this question ["What is man?"] to themselves, to become aware that the answer is neither obvious nor simply unavailable, and that there is no serious life in which this question is not a continuous concern. Despite all the efforts to pervert it, the question that every young person asks, "Who am I?," the powerful urge to follow the Delphic command, "Know thyself," which is born in each of us, means in the first place "What is man?" And in our chronic lack of certainty, this comes down to knowing the alternative answers and thinking about them. Liberal education provides access to these alternatives, many of which go against the grain of our nature or our times. The liberally educated person is one who is able to resist the easy and preferred answers, not because he is obstinate but because he knows others worthy of consideration.[2]

Bloom's book still reverberates across higher education, precisely because the battle he fought still rages today. Debates over the ideological preferences of universities in general, and faculty in particular, are a constant on cable news. I have avoided this debate not because it isn't important, but because it detracts from our purpose. Indeed, Bloom would likely criticize what he would call my "utilitarian" approach to higher education. Under this view, the four years one spends at college are a time for intense philosophical scrutiny of one's place in the world, using as a guide the great texts of human history. To put it in a less grandiose way, Bloom would argue that the study of these classical works prepares the young mind for a lifetime of critical thinking and learning—two traits that would serve one well in any profession.

I don't disagree. By no means do I believe the study of liberal arts to be anything less than a noble, worthwhile pursuit. But the idea that this is the only acceptable role of higher education is a relic of a bygone age, when only elite students had the opportunity to attend college. In those days, college was reserved for a small minority who didn't go to college to prepare them for a career, unless that career was in academia.

The purpose of college has changed because the number and type of students who now attend college has grown. For some of these students, the liberal arts are ideally suited to their goals and temperaments. But for most other students, they go to college to improve their lives, seek opportunities, and get a degree that opens doors. It would be a disservice to these students to adhere to an old-fashioned view of college that prizes the liberal arts above all else.

My advice to you is simple: use your four years at college as wisely as you can. You have a lifetime to learn and pursue intellectual interests. There are many tools available to the lifelong student that weren't available to students of Bloom's time. I would encourage you to use them. By studying the liberal arts, you will discover a richness and depth to life that you can only glimpse today. You will learn to think critically and wisely. After all, Peter Thiel was a philosophy major.

But also know that the college experience has changed because the economy has changed. There are skills you must have to compete successfully in this new economy. College will help you acquire these skills, if you approach your studies with some forethought. My attempt with this chapter was to provide some guidance to your four years, but what you do now is entirely your choice. Just remember that these four years are ones you will never get back: live them well.

ELEVEN

The Internship

In recent years, there have been two popular movies based on a similar premise. In one, called *The Internship*, Owen Wilson and Vince Vaughn play out-of-work watch salesmen whose prospects for finding another job in their field look grim. Instead, the two forty-something friends devise a scheme to apply to the coveted internship program at Google. The other movie, called *The Intern*, isn't much different, except the "displaced worker" role is played by a much older Robert De Niro, who interns for the founder and CEO of an e-commerce fashion startup. In both films, hilarity ensues as the middle-aged or senior interns interact with their much, much younger peers.

It's no coincidence that both movies came out within a few years of each other. The economic dilemma behind the plot of each movie is very real and not nearly as funny as the movies themselves. Worker displacement is when employees in a company or industry lose their jobs permanently because the job doesn't exist anymore. Technology is usually the culprit, though not always. Workers in this category must get trained for a new job, which is not easy, especially when you're above a certain age. The stars in these movies recognize that the only way they can find work is if they learn the skills rewarded by the new economy—i.e., skills that are useful to a tech company.

What's interesting is that the movies assume that the place one goes to first learn these new skills is at an internship. And in a way, they're right. The most valuable experience you can get before you are actually working is at an internship. What's more, the absolute best time to get this type of experience is *before you graduate*. Far too many recent college graduates wait until after they've thrown their caps in the air to start their internships. Better late than never, but many internships are unpaid. This is less than ideal because the moment you step off the college campus, you will have only a brief grace period before the bank starts sending you student loan statements. When you step off campus, it's far better to be stepping into your first job, rather than into an unpaid internship.

A 2014 survey from Pew Research sheds light on this issue:

> [T]he Pew Research survey asked college graduates whether, while still in school, they could have better prepared for the type of job they wanted by gaining more work experience, studying harder or beginning their job search earlier.
>
> About three-quarters of all college graduates say taking at least one of those steps would have enhanced their chances to land their ideal job. Leading the should-have-done list: getting more work experience while still in school. *Half say taking this step would have put them in a better position to get the kind of job they wanted.* About four-in-ten (38%) regret not studying harder, while three-in-ten say they should have started looking for a job sooner (30%) or picked a different major (29%). [Emphasis added][1]

This is where the internship comes in. By far, an internship in college is the single best way to improve your job prospects after graduation. It also will give you the type of hands-on, real-life experience that we try very hard to emulate at Project Lead The Way. Our philosophy has always been that the earlier students can see subjects applied in a real-world work environment, the more serious and dedicated they will be about their studies. And the reverse is also true: learning what you don't like doing is just as important as learning what you do like. For example, if you thought you had a passion for biotechnology only to discover that you dislike your summer internship at a pharmaceutical lab, wouldn't you want to know that before you graduated college?

But I'll let you hear it from those same recent college graduates you met earlier—Quinn, Juliana, and Mark. As you'll see, all three place a great deal of credit for their after-college successes on their college internships. Let's get to it.

IT'S NEVER TOO EARLY

You might remember that Quinn is an electrical engineer for Chevron. He does the sort of things you probably wouldn't expect from someone under thirty, like managing hundred-million-dollar projects around the globe. What you might not remember is that Quinn also worked for Chevron during his internships in college. He explains:

> The first summer after my freshman year [in college] I knew I wanted to get an internship somewhere. I wasn't ready to go home just quite yet, because I was still eager to learn and build upon my skill set. I knew the importance of internships going

into college, and they talked about it throughout our freshman orientation. The message was: "This is something you should do." My first industry internship with Chevron was in 2009, where I really learned about the engineering design process. These are the things you don't learn in the classroom: how you conduct design research; how you get from point A, to B, and C.

For me it was an exciting moment. I had already begun to bridge the gap between classroom theory and practical application, but now I saw the theories applied in an industry setting. Everything I had learned up to that point would be tested or validated through that summer internship. And Chevron treated us like a member of the team: we were ranked as employees and compared amongst our peers. We were dealing with real dollars, and real Chevron capital.

After that first summer, Chevron offered me another internship after my sophomore year, in summer 2010. After that internship I received my full-time offer before even starting my senior year. For me, that offer took a lot of pressure off of my shoulders. Of course my parents were patting themselves on the back! They were like, "Well, our job is done: he's got a job before he even graduates!"

I hope you picked up on a few things from Quinn's internship. First, I hope you saw that Quinn went into college knowing he wanted to get an internship *as soon as possible*. Far too many college students think that the internship is only after their sophomore year, or perhaps junior year, like it's something to be checked off. "There! Did my internship, now I can go work as a lifeguard by the beach."

Rather, Quinn formed a relationship with his future employers at Chevron. They worked with him; got to know him; and they saw his passion and commitment to the field. The only "job interview" Quinn ever had was for that first internship. Every other opportunity at Chevron was *offered* to him.

Second, I hope you noticed how Quinn mentioned an "industry setting." What do you think he means by that? Just this: you learn how the science works in the classroom and see the science come alive in the lab. But, really, what have you seen other than just a really cool demonstration? What is *marketable* about this particular use of science? How can a company turn this piece of science into something *useful*? This is what Quinn meant by "industry setting." He didn't just see the science come alive; he saw the science at work, doing things that made a real difference in the lives of millions of people. And he learned all of this before he got his first Chevron paycheck.

THE PEOPLE FACTOR

Throughout your career, you're going to have to work 'ith other people. This might seem insultingly obvious to , but it's important to really consider how relationships human interaction are inseparable from working. deed, many will tell you that knowing how to work well with your peers, your team, and your bosses is the most important part of any job. It certainly is the most interesting. The reason I mention this now is because an internship brings you face-to-face with this major element of adult life: the reality of working side-by-side with others.

It's a lesson Juliana learned from her internship days at GE. You might remember that Juliana, who excelled at STEM subjects at a very early age, eventually decided to become an educator with PLTW. But I'll let her tell the story:

> During my college summers I had two internships with GE. One was more technical, while the other was more operations focused. But what I really loved was being right there on the shop floor watching the work. GE Aviation is the world's leading provider of jet engines, so when I first interned at GE, I walked into this giant, unglamorous building. Really, it looked like something out of a movie. Except, when you walk in and turn a corner, there's a row of F414 engines, which go

into FA18s, like the Blue Angels. That was just like, "Wow, this is incredible." You sit in class and talk about these things, but to see it, to see it made, to literally meet the people who made all the engines in the country that go into this aircraft, that was just incredible. It definitely translated into what I wanted to do for work.

I had realized by then I had strong technical skills, but what I really enjoyed were the interactions that were required to put those skills into action. I did not want to be the engineer doing CAD drawings all day long. I certainly learned a lot of new, practical skills during the more technical internship; but it was through the operations internship that I learned the "people skills." I wanted to be more hands-on, and I realized that's where I stood out amongst my peers was really with the people skills that I had developed. I don't like the term "soft skills," but those first entry skills pulled me in a different direction.

Those two internships basically turned into a job. I was hired in September of my senior year; almost a full year before I was to begin I already had the job. GE's really heavy on internally recruiting from their interns. I was interviewed in August before my senior year even started, and by September I had my offer letter.

In addition to her GE internships, Juliana also volunteered for PLTW during her summers at college. Given what Juliana ended up doing, both work experiences were equally important for her future success.

In her interactions with others, in learning the operations side of a company, Juliana discovered some talents she didn't know she possessed. Or perhaps she never considered that these "soft skills" (professional skills) were particularly relevant to her career and job aspirations. But that's why the internship is an experience unlike any other you can have in college; the things you learn about yourself, the good and the bad, will shine a light on opportunities you never considered before. And, again, you will also learn what you're not particularly good at—and this rarely has anything to do with knowledge or skills. Some people, no matter how hard they try, will never make good executives, because they have no knack for managing people. You can read all you want about management styles and leading a team, but until you try it, you won't know if you can do it. And that means getting out of the classroom when you're still a student.

KNOCKING ON DOORS OPENS THEM

You might recall that Mark, who's an engineer for Lockheed Martin, often speaks to high school students about engineering. Part of Mark's story is that he wasn't all that gifted in math. It took Mark a lot of hard work to earn the grades that allowed him to pursue his dream of becoming an engineer. Obviously, this is a story that Mark loves to tell high schoolers, many of whom probably never considered an engineering career because they believed they were bad at math. So when I asked Mark to give me an example of the sort of things he says to these high schoolers, he answered:

> I always start out by asking: "Who in here is fantastic at math?" Of course usually only two people raise their hand, which lets me say: "Well, that doesn't mean you can't be an engineer. If you guys take anything away from today, it's know that you don't have to be a genius, and you don't have to be perfect. If you get an engineering degree, you'll probably always find a job. *And you have to have an internship*." [Emphasis added]
>
> An internship is the difference between a guy that engineers the feet on washing machines and the guy who is doing air combat analysis at Lockheed Martin, which is the difference between me and a couple of my friends. No internships: They got by, and they got their degree. But they weren't knocking on doors. And so one of my buddies, he's literally doing the drawings for feet on washing machines. Actually, he's not even doing the

drawings; he's looking at the drawings of the guys who do it. So you're the low man on the totem pole.

Of course it's easier said than done. I knew that I wanted to get an internship in college but I just couldn't get one to save my life. I didn't have the grades to get into the more competitive programs and I just didn't really know anyone who could help me find one. That's kind of how Lockheed is: Almost no one gets in the door without knowing somebody.

I always knew I wanted to do something in aerospace because I have a lot of family that worked for Lockheed. It was a pretty lucky deal, but in high school everyone knew me as "[the] one who takes all those engineering classes." This was my reputation in high school, if you can believe it. So when I was in college, an old high school classmate called me out of the blue and said, "Hey, I know you used to study engineering in high school, didn't you?" I said, "Yeah. I still do right now at the University of North Texas."

She says, "My sister works at Airbus Helicopters and she's looking for an intern." I was like, "Throw my name in there!" Then it was all about her just putting me in touch. But the thing was the internship was open to anyone, meaning that the people who applied had already graduated college; they already had engineering degrees! I didn't think I had much of a chance, but during the interview I mentioned Project Lead The Way. It just so happened my future boss knew all about PLTW and it spoke volumes to him.

That's how I got my first internship. It just fell into my lap.

I think Mark is being a little too humble. The Airbus internship, which would lead to a job at Lockheed Martin, didn't just fall into his lap. He worked for it. He went after it. He approached college with a plan to get an internship.

If you've picked up on nothing else, I hope you've seen the importance of *thinking ahead*. Mark thought ahead and was open to any opportunity. But if Mark were like your average sophomore in college, he wouldn't have jumped on the random opportunity his old high school classmate offered him.

The other lesson from Mark's internship story is to get creative. He struck out with several traditional internship programs. But that didn't deter him. He kept after it until he found one. Don't make the mistake of thinking this is a minor point. "Getting creative" in your career decisions, even before you have a career, is a major factor in realizing your dreams. You must approach your search for an internship with the same intensity you will approach your job search after college. As you have seen, that first internship can lead to your first job. But more than that, you will learn your first lesson about life in the new economy: although there is always going to be someone better, smarter, or more well-connected than you are, you can compete with determination, discipline, and hard work.

As you'll see, many universities offer course credit for certain internships, while other majors require them. But if yours doesn't, then it's up to you to find one on your own. Your university should help you in your search. But don't rely solely on your university to do the searching. It's up to you to find the right experience for your passion. Universities and colleges do a good job of guiding their students competently through their four years, but they won't hold your hand. You can't simply sign up for the right courses, make good grades, and expect the job offers to start rolling in. Employers won't come to you unless they know about you first.

And the best way for them to know about you? The internship.

TWELVE

The Three Answers

started this book with a story about a student who asked his trigonometry teacher a good question: "Why do we need to learn this?" Unfortunately, the teacher didn't have a good answer.

We now know that you don't learn trigonometry in case you want to become a high school math teacher. You learn trigonometry in case you want to become a mechanical engineer, an electrical engineer, a civil engineer, an architect, a draftsman, a structural engineer, a pilot, an astronomer, a physicist, a communications engineer, a computer graphics artist, or a game developer. And this is to just name the most obvious jobs and careers that require trigonometry.

High school students rarely have the opportunity to connect their studies to real-world jobs. They have some vague notion that the reason they learn trigonometry is because that's what an educated person should know. A mediocre math student, however, won't work harder on his trig homework just because he wants to be an "educated person."

But he might work harder if he knew that trigonometry is an essential part of video game design. Even if he wasn't going to win any awards in mathematics, he would still want to learn exactly what he needed to know to become a game developer.

Right now, too many students do it backwards. They don't learn trigonometry because they want to do something that requires trig; they first see if they're good at trig, then they decide whether to do something with it. This method assumes that our innate talents should play the dominant role in deciding our career. But why should that be the case? Why should we limit our dreams only to those fields in which we have a natural talent?

You now know that you don't have to. You *will* learn trig—or biology—or coding—or composition—if your determination to achieve your dream is strong enough. You *will* learn your hardest subject because you know that entering college with a plan is the best way to leave college with a job. Even if you don't know what you want to do, you now know the things that will help you find a job after college in most any field. Study and learn those subjects for *that* reason. Learn something about computer science because most companies are turning into computer-focused, tech-based companies.

But the student's question about trig isn't the only one you heard from the first chapter. We can answer the other questions I asked now too.

WHAT IS YOUR DREAM?

You know that whatever dream you have now might change after further investigation or study. You know that your dreams are limited by your experiences and, frankly, you simply don't have enough experiences to say that you know *exactly* what you want to do with the rest of your life. That is not to say that your dream must change; only that you must be open to changing it.

You know that your dream will change when you actively seek out the connections between school and career. Unless someone in your family builds jet engines, it's unlikely you've ever thought of building jet engines for a living. But plenty of teenagers want to be pilots for a living. And now you know that even if you don't become a pilot, you can still have a career in the field of your dreams, aviation. You can still be a part of those magnificent machines and the industry of flying them.

You know that whatever you're good at in school doesn't have to decide what you do after school. You know that as good as you are at a particular subject, you aren't defined by or limited to these talents. You know that you cannot let your talents or lack of talent dictate your life. You know that being bad at a subject in middle or high school doesn't mean you can't pursue a career that uses that subject. You know that not every engineer who works at Lockheed Martin was an A math student. You know that you need to be competent at a subject, which might require a lot of hard work and extra hours, but by no means do you need to be a master at it.

You know that when you talk about your "dream" you don't mean a single job. You mean a career in a field or profession that allows you to change and adapt to the shifting demands of the economy—as well as your own preferences and career needs. But you know that when you pick the right dream for you, it will allow you to build a set of skills that should last a lifetime.

WILL YOU BE READY FOR THIS RAPIDLY EVOLVING WORLD?

You now know that the financial realities of the world beyond adolescence hit you the day you graduate college. You know that the best way to prepare for that reality—to leave college in the best possible position to face that reality—is to start today. You now know financial distress is a dream killer. You understand that you aren't too young to start preparing to be financially secure.

You also know that the world economy is not the one your parents entered when they left school. It won't even be the one college seniors are entering today. The rise of digital data and technology means that the economy remakes itself every few years. But you also know that the trend is clear: in time, nearly every company will be a tech company. You know that Google is making cars and General Motors is making computers for cars. This tells you what sort of skills will be in demand in tomorrow's economy. You know that you can't predict the future, but you can certainly prepare for it.

Above all, you know that when someone asks you this or something similar—what do you want to do?—you know what to say. You want to provide *value*. You know that a bachelor's degree is necessary but also isn't enough. You know that employers are frustrated with the quality of graduates leaving college, because they are unprepared for the realities of the economy. Employers need someone who can do the job on Day One. And you know what skills are most likely to put you ahead of your peers. You know that the worst thing that you can be after you graduate college is a commodity.

WHAT DO YOU WANT TO GET OUT OF COLLEGE?

You know that you should choose a college for financial reasons as much as for quality reasons. You know that beyond the Top Twenty-Five schools, employers will care more about what you learned at college than where you went to college. You know that choosing the right college has less to do with how high the college is ranked than whether it will provide you with the right courses at the right price.

You know that you can spend four, or five, or six years at college and graduate with a degree, but that this doesn't mean you're ready. You know that college is dreadfully expensive, but that you're also buying something. You understand that every single class you attend (or don't) costs money. You know that you want to get something for your money.

You also know that you can't simply fulfill the requirements for your major. You know that even as industries are slowly converging, colleges still teach courses separately; that a math major won't be required to learn composition and an English major won't be required to learn computer science. You know that this puts the responsibility on you to fill the gaps of your major; that the critical skills you need to be valuable to employers are skills you can—and should—learn in your elective courses.

You know that for all that you learn in the classroom, nothing beats the experience of real life. You know that finding the right internship is the single best thing you can do during your college career to improve your job search after graduation. You've seen how the right internship—which you should get as soon as possible—leads to the right job. You've seen how the right work experience either confirms the path you've chosen or signals a course correction. You know that the best time to change your mind isn't when the student loan bills start coming in, but before you've stepped off campus.

In other words, you now know why you go to college. You go to college to learn the skills and acquire the knowledge that will serve you for the rest of your life. You go to college to strengthen the innate talents and abilities you have but which aren't enough to set you apart from your peers. You go to college to differentiate yourself—to be more than just a college graduate. You go to college to learn what you need to know to live the life you want.

Finally, you know that the only "wrong" dream is the one left unexamined. So go examine your dream. Then go live it.

Acknowledgments

During a recent school visit a curious fifth grader asked me a profound question: "What keeps you up at night?" I paused for a moment before responding, "You do." And it is my concern about his, along with 54 million other students in the United States, ability to develop the knowledge and skills to thrive in our rapidly changing global economy that inspired this book.

However, this book would not have been possible without the immense contributions and support of my great family, friends, and colleagues.

Each day I am inspired by the tireless commitment of the PLTW team, our board of directors, and our many partners who all care deeply about the success of America's students and teachers. Thank you!

Thank you to the extraordinarily talented Blake Dvorak for his great work, insights, and support throughout this journey.

Thank you to the great team at the Pinkston Group for their ongoing support, and to my colleagues Kiley Adolph, Rex Bolinger, Lauren Curtis, Jonathan Dilley, David Dimmett, Jennifer Cahill Erbacher, Carol Killworth, Tom Luna, and Natasha Richardson O'Neill whose input helped shape the final manuscript.

Finally, thank you to my wonderful family, Jill, Josh, Ryan, Drew, and Riley for their unconditional love and support. I am proud of each of you.

Vince M. Bertram
Indianapolis, Indiana
July 2017

Notes

ONE: THE THREE QUESTIONS

1. David Langdon et. al, "STEM: Good Jobs Now and for the Future," U.S. Department of Commerce, Economics and Statistics Administration, July 2011, http://www.esa.doc.gov/sites/default/files/stemfinalyjuly14_1.pdf.

TWO: DO YOU HAVE A DREAM?

1. Melissa Kirk, "The Problem with 'Follow Your Dreams,'" *Psychology Today*, April 2, 2013, https://www.psychologytoday.com/blog/test-case/201304/the-problem-follow-your-dreams-0.

2. Jenny Wong and Bryony Jones, "What's the perfect job for you? Ask your five-year-old self," CNN, January 28, 2015, http://www.cnn.com/2015/01/28/europe/perfect-job-career-childhood/.

3. Lindsay Gellman, "Millennials: Love Them or Let Them Go," *Wall Street Journal*, May 6, 2015, http://www.wsj.com/articles/how-employers-wrangle-restless-millennials-1430818203

FOUR: DREAMS IN ACTION

1. Alan Neuhauser and Lindsey Cook, "2016 U.S. News/Raytheon STEM Index Shows Uptick in Hiring, Education," *U.S. News & World Report*, May 17, 2016, https://www.usnews.com/news/articles/2016-05-17/the-new-stem-index-2016.

2. Ibid.

FIVE: THE WORLD DOESN'T CARE ABOUT YOUR DREAMS

1. Quentin Fottrell, "Half of College Graduates Expect to Be Supported by Their Families," Marketwatch, published in *New York Post*, May 19, 2015, http://nypost.com/2015/05/19/half-of-college-graduates-expect-to-be-supported-by-their-families/.

2. Jeffrey M. Jones, "In U.S., 14% of Those Aged 24 to 34 Are Living With Parents," Gallup, February 13, 2014, http://www.gallup.com/poll/167426/aged-living-parents.aspx.

3. Tomikka Anderson, "Cost of Average San Francisco Rent Actually Fell (a Little) Last Month," *San Francisco Chronicle*, December 11, 2015, http://www.sfgate.com/bayarea/article/San-Francisco-rent-cost-drop-rental-6690357.php.

4. "Salary Survey Executive Summary," National Association of Colleges and Employers (Spring 2016), http://www.naceweb.org/uploadedfiles/content/static-assets/downloads/executive-summary/2016-spring-salary-survey-executive-summary.pdf.

5. "Tuition costs of colleges and universities," Fast Facts, National Center for Education Statistics, http://nces.ed.gov/fastfacts/display.asp?id=76.

6. "Quick Facts about Student Debt," The Institute for College Access & Success, March 2014, http://ticas.org/sites/default/files/pub_files/Debt_Facts_and_Sources.pdf.

7. Blake Ellis, "40 Million Americans Now Have Student Loan Debt," CNN Money, September 10, 2014, http://money.cnn.com/2014/09/10/pf/college/student-loans/.

8. Victor Luckerson, "The Myth of the Four-Year College Degree," *Time*, January 10, 2013, http://business.time.com/2013/01/10/the-myth-of-the-4-year-college-degree/.

9. Danielle Douglas-Gabriel, "Why So Many Students Are Spending Six Years Getting a College Degree,"

Washington Post, December 2, 2014, http://www. washingtonpost.com/blogs/wonkblog/wp/2014/12/02/ why-so-many-students-are-spending-six-years-getting- a-college-degree/.

10. Master of Fine Arts (MFA) Degree Average Salary, Payscale, updated March 25, 2017, http://www. payscale.com/research/US/Degree=Master_of_Fine_ Arts_(MFA)/Salary#by_Years_Experience.

11. Jaison R. Abel, Richard Deitz, and Yaqin Su, "Are Recent College Graduates Finding Good Jobs?" *Current Issues in Economics and Finances* 20, no. 1 (2014), http://www.newyorkfed.org/research/current_ issues/ci20-1.pdf.

12. Jordan Weismann, "How Bad is the Job Market for the College Class of 2014?" *Slate*, May 8, 2014, http:// www.slate.com/blogs/moneybox/2014/05/08/ unemployment_and_the_class_of_2014_how_bad_is_ the_job_market_for_new_college.html.

SIX: IT'S NOT YOUR PARENTS' ECONOMY

1. "Traffic Fatalities Fall in 2014, But Early Estimates Show 2015 Trending Higher," National Highway Traffic Safety Administration, November 24, 2015, https://www.nhtsa.gov/press-releases/traffic-fatalities- fall-2014-early-estimates-show-2015-trending-higher.

2. Murali Krishnan, "India has the highest number of road accidents in the world," *Deutsch Welle*, April 29,

2010, http://www.dw.com/en/india-has-the-highest-number-of-road-accidents-in-the-world/a-5519345; Elizabeth Whitman, "China Traffic Deaths: More Than 200,00 Annual Fatilities In Road Accidents, World Health Organization Says," *International Business Times* May 6, 2015, http://www.ibtimes.com/china-traffic-deaths-more-200000-annual-fatilities-road-accidents-world-health-1910537.

3. SINTEF, "Big Data, for better or worse: 90% of world's data generated over last two years," *ScienceDaily*, May 22, 2013, https://www.sciencedaily.com/releases/2013/05/130522085217.htm.

4. Shawn DuBravac, *Digital Destiny: How the New Age of Data Will Transform the Way We Work, Live, and Communicate* (Washington, DC: Regnery Publishing, 2015).

5. Rita McGrath, "The Pace of Technology Adoption is Speeding Up," Harvard Business Review, November 25, 2013, https://hbr.org/2013/11/the-pace-of-technology-adoption-is-speeding-up/.

6. Michael DeGusta, "Are Smart Phones Spreading Faster than Any Technology in Human History?" *MIT Technology Review*, May 9, 2012, https://www.technologyreview.com/s/427787/are-smart-phones-spreading-faster-than-any-technology-in-human-history/.

7. "Available Locally, Expanding Globally," Uber Newsroom, https://newsroom.uber.com/locations/.

8. Lee Ohanian and Edward Prescott, "Behind the Productivity Plunge: Fewer Startups," *Wall Street Journal*, June 25, 2014, http://www.wsj.com/articles/behind-the-productivity-plunge-fewer-startups-1403737197.

9. Ibid.

10. John Dearie and Courtney Geduldig, *Where the Jobs Are*: *Entrepreneurship and the Soul of the American Economy* (Hoboken, NJ: Wiley, 2013).

11. Ibid.

12. Ibid.

13. Scott Jaschik, "Well-Prepared in Their Own Eyes," *Inside Higher Ed*, January 20, 2015, https://www.insidehighered.com/news/2015/01/20/study-finds-big-gaps-between-student-and-employer-perceptions.

SEVEN: WHERE TO FIND JOBS

1. Jonathan Rothwell, *The Hidden STEM Economy*, Brookings, June 10, 2013, https://www.brookings.edu/research/the-hidden-stem-economy/.

2. Jonathan Rothwell, *Still Searching*: *Job Vacancies and STEM Skills*, Brookings, July 1, 2014, http://texhilltech.weebly.com/uploads/5/3/6/2/53626753/still_searching__job_vacancies_and_stem_skills___brookings_institution.pdf, 2.

3. Government Accountability Office, *Science, Technology, Engineering, and Mathematics Education: Assessing the Relationship between Education and the Workforce*, May 2014, https://www.gao.gov/assets/670/663079.pdf.

4. Vital Signs and Change the Equation, "Where the Jobs Are: In STEM Fields," in *Scientific American*, https://www.scientificamerican.com/mediakit/assets/File/topoftheagenda_STEM.pdf.

5. Ibid.

6. "Dow and Project Lead the Way Partner to Grow STEM Skills in Key Dow Communities," PLTW Press Release, February 24, 2015, https://www.pltw.org/news/dow-and-project-lead-the-way-partner-to-grow-stem-skills-in-key-dow-communities.

7. Bureau of Labor Statistics, "Table A-4: Employment status of the civilian population 25 years and over by educational attainment," Economic News Release, https://www.bls.gov/news.release/empsit.t04.htm.

8. William J. Bennett and David Wilezol, *Is College Worth It? A Former United States Secretary of Education and a Liberal Arts Graduate Expose the Broken Promise of Higher Education* (New York: HarperCollins, 2013), vii.

9. Michael Grothaus, "The Top Jobs in 10 Years Might Not Be What You Expect," *Fast Company*, May 18,

2015, https://www.fastcompany.com/3046277/the-top-jobs-in-10-years-might-not-be-what-you-expect.

10. Ibid.

11. Ibid.

12. Ibid.

13. Jonathan Rothwell and Siddarth Kulkarni, *Beyond College Rankings: A Value-Added Approach to Assessing Two- and Four-Year Schools*, Brookings Metropolitan Policy Program, April 2015, https://www.brookings.edu/wp-content/uploads/2015/04/BMPP_CollegeValueAdded.pdf.

14. Sam Parr, "New Study: Ivy League Grads Earn Less Than Less Prestigious Colleges," *The Hustle*, October 7, 2015, https://thehustle.co/new-study-ivy-league-grads-earn-less-than-less-prestigious-colleges/.

15. Annalyn Censky, "4 Degrees with 0% Unemployment," *CNN Money*, May 23, 2012, http://money.cnn.com/galleries/2012/news/economy/1205/gallery.high-demand-jobs/index.html.

16. Anthony P. Carnevale, Ban Cheah, and Andrew R. Hanson, *The Economic Value of College Majors*, Georgetown University Center on Education and the Workforce," 2015, https://cew.georgetown.edu/cew-reports/valueofcollegemajors/#explore-data.

17. Brookings Institution, "Metro Monitor 2017 Dashboard," February 23, 2017, https://www.brookings.edu/interactives/metro-monitor-2017-dashboard/.

18. Ibid.

19. Chevron Sponsor Content, "The Jobs of Today," *The Atlantic*, http://www.theatlantic.com/sponsored/chevron-stem-education/the-jobs-of-today/196/.

20. William Levitan, "Letter to the Editor: What STEM Education Teaches," *The Washington Post*, April 3, 2015, https://www.washingtonpost.com/opinions/what-stem-education-teaches/2015/04/03/74a88fcc-d700-11e4-bf0b-f648b95a6488_story.html?utm_term=.5f69304ac578.

EIGHT: DON'T BE A COMMODITY

1. Richard Gunderman and Mark Mutz, "The Collapse of Big Law: A Cautionary Tale for Big Med," *The Atlantic*, February 11, 2014, https://www.theatlantic.com/business/archive/2014/02/the-collapse-of-big-law-a-cautionary-tale-for-big-med/283736/.

2. Elizabeth Olson, "Law Graduate Gets Her Day in Court, Suing Law School," *The New York Times*, March 6, 2016, https://www.nytimes.com/2016/03/07/business/dealbook/court-to-hear-suit-accusing-law-school-of-inflating-job-data.html.

3. Benjamin H. Barton, "The Fall and Rise of Lawyers," *CNN*, May 23, 2015, http://www.cnn.com/2015/05/22/opinions/barton-rise-and-fall-of-lawyers/.

4. Kathleen Klink, MD, "Incentives for Physicians to Pursue Primary Care in the ACA Era," *AMA Journal of Ethics* 17 no. 7 (July 2015), http://journalofethics.ama-assn.org/2015/07/stas1-1507.html.

5. Tim Dall et al., *2016 Update: The Complexities of Physician Supply and Demand: Projections from 2014 to 2025*, Association of American Medical Colleges, April 5, 2016, https://www.aamc.org/download/458082/data/2016_complexities_of_supply_and_demand_projections.pdf.

6. Jennifer LeClaire, "Adobe Rolls Out New Data Visualization Tool," *Sci-Tech Today*, September 5, 2015, http://www.sci-tech-today.com/news/Adobe-Rolls-Out-New-Data-Viz-Tool/story.xhtml?story_id=12200DMHNPDI.

NINE: WHY COLLEGE?

1. "Thiel Foundation Announces 2015 Thiel Fellows, Expands Fellowship Program," Business Wire, June 5, 2015, http://www.businesswire.com/news/home/20150605005092/en/Thiel-Foundation-Announces-2015-Thiel-Fellows-Expands.

2. Mick Brown, "Peter Thiel: the Billionaire Tech Entrepreneur on a Mission to Cheat Death," *The Telegraph*, September 19, 2014, http://www.telegraph. co.uk/technology/11098971/Peter-Thiel-the-billionaire-tech-entrepreneur-on-a-mission-to-cheat-death.html.

3. Valerie Strauss, "Steve Jobs Told Students: 'Stay Hungry. Stay foolish,'" *The Washington Post*, October 5, 2011, https://www.washingtonpost.com/blogs/answer-sheet/post/steve-jobs-told-students-stay-hungry-stay-foolish/2011/10/05/gIQA1qVjOL_blog.html?utm_term=.68e19b77f262.

4. Eduardo Porter, "Dropping Out of College, and Paying the Price," *The New York Times*, June 25, 2013, http://www.nytimes.com/2013/06/26/business/economy/dropping-out-of-college-and-paying-the-price.html.

5. "The Rising Cost of Not Going to College," Pew Research Center, February 11, 2014, http://www.pewsocialtrends.org/2014/02/11/the-rising-cost-of-not-going-to-college/.

6. Mary C. Daly and Yifan Cao, "Does College Pay?" Federal Reserve Bank of San Francisco 2014 Annual Report, http://sffed-education.org/annualreport2014/files/2014%20Annual%20Report%20Daly%2004%2021%202015.pdf.

7. David Leonhardt, "Is College Worth It? Clearly, New Data Say," *The New York Times*, May 27, 2014,

https://www.nytimes.com/2014/05/27/upshot/
is-college-worth-it-clearly-new-data-say.html.

TEN: YOUR FOUR YEARS

1. "Four-Year Myth: Make College More Affordable. Restore the Promise of Graduating on Time," Complete College America, 2014, http://completecollege.org/wp-content/uploads/2014/11/4-Year-Myth.pdf.
2. Allan Bloom, *The Closing of the American Mind* (New York: Simon & Schuster, 1988), 21.

ELEVEN: THE INTERNSHIP

1. "The Rising Cost of Not Going to College," Pew Research Center, February 11, 2014, http://www.pewsocialtrends.org/2014/02/11/the-rising-cost-of-not-going-to-college/.